California Natural History Guides: 12

BUTTERFLIES

OF THE

SAN FRANCISCO BAY REGION

BY

J. W. TILDEN

ILLUSTRATIONS BY GENE M. CHRISTMAN

UNIVERSITY OF CALIFORNIA PRESS
BERKELEY, LOS ANGELES, LONDON

UNIVERSITY OF CALIFORNIA PRESS
BERKELEY AND LOS ANGELES, CALIFORNIA

UNIVERSITY OF CALIFORNIA PRESS LTD.
LONDON, ENGLAND

SECOND PRINTING, 1974
ISBN: 0–520–01268–2
LIBRARY OF CONGRESS CATALOG CARD NUMBER: 64-24888
PRINTED IN THE UNITED STATES OF AMERICA

CONTENTS

Of the 682 North American butterflies, 122 have been recorded from the San Francisco Bay region. Eight of the ten families of the Nearctic Region are found here. The only butterfly families not represented in our area are the Libytheidae, represented by two North American species ranging from Arizona to the Atlantic coast and up to Canada in the east, and the Megathymidae, consisting of several yucca-boring skippers confined to the area from southern California to Florida.

Our local butterflies vary in size from the tiny Pygmy Blue *(Brephidium exilis)*, one of the world's smallest butterflies with a wingspread of less than one-half inch, to the Two-tailed Swallowtail *(Papilio multicaudata)*, with a wingspread of from four to six inches.

With the help of this volume you may learn where to find our Bay region butterflies and their caterpillars; how to identify them; how to study them and record your observations; and how to make a butterfly collection. Sources of additional information are provided for those who may wish to delve more deeply into the subject.

Information is provided for all 122 species recorded from the San Francisco Bay region and a handy check-list which doubles as an index to species accounts and illustrations is included. Nearly all species are illustrated; 70 in color, and the others in black and white.

[5]

Although butterflies are among the most conspicuous of insects there are many gaps in our knowledge of the details of the habits and life histories of even many of our common species. Thus such terms as "early stages unknown" or "food plant not recorded" many occur all too frequently in the accounts to follow. For this reason even the beginner may be able to make worthwhile contributions to science through keeping careful records of his observations of our San Francisco Bay region butterflies and their caterpillars.

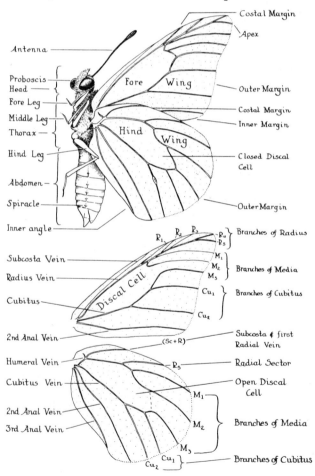

WHAT ARE BUTTERFLIES?

Butterflies and moths are closely related. Together they make up the order Lepidoptera, which means "scaly-wings." If you examine the "powder" which will come off if you touch a butterfly or moth wing, you will see why they were given this name. You will see overlapping rows of scales, somewhat like those of a fish in appearance. Each butterfly has its own distinctive scale shape and arrangement (see below).

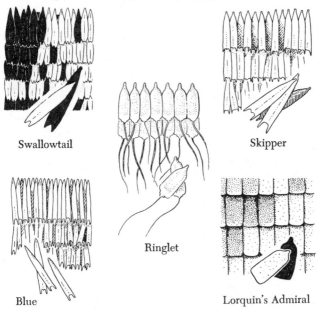

Swallowtail

Skipper

Ringlet

Blue

Lorquin's Admiral

You may wonder how to tell a butterfly from a moth. All butterflies normally fly in the daytime and most moths fly at night. However, there are many day-flying moths that could be mistaken for butterflies. You may think of butterflies as slender-bodied, brightly-colored insects, and moths as heavy-bodied and dull-colored.

[7]

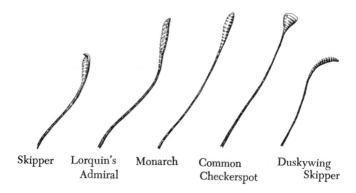

Skipper   Lorquin's   Monarch   Common   Duskywing
           Admiral   Checkerspot   Skipper

However this does not really serve to distinguish them for you may find quite a number of slender-bodied, brightly colored moths as well as some butterflies that are heavy-bodied and dull-colored. The most convenient method of telling butterflies from moths is by looking at the feelers or antennae. Butterfly feelers are swollen at the tip into a knob or club (see above). Moth antennae may be thread-like, comb-like or feather-shaped, but not clubbed.

The body of a butterfly, like that of all insects, is composed of three sections — head, thorax, and abdomen. The head bears the mouthparts, antennae, and the eyes.

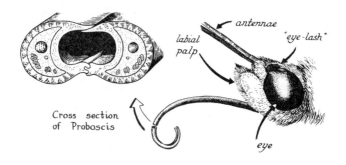

antennae

labial
palp

"eye-lash"

Cross section
of Proboscis

eye

The mouthparts of adult butterflies form a sucking tube, coiled like a watch spring. One antenna projects forward from each side of the head. The eyes of a butterfly are large and composed of many little eyes called facets. Butterfly eyes are good for perceiving movement and are also able to see color.

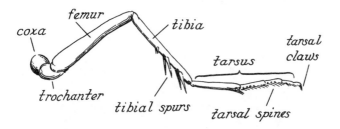

The thorax, the section immediately behind the head, is composed of three segments, each of which bears a pair of legs. The second and third segments of the thorax each bear a pair of wings as well. The front wings are usually much larger than the hind wings.

The abdomen does not bear either legs or wings. At the tip of the abdomen are located the external reproductive organs, and inside the abdomen are the digestive organs and the internal reproductive organs.

In growing up, the butterfly passes through four stages. The change in form from one stage to another is called *metamorphosis*.

The life of a butterfly begins with an egg. Many butterfly eggs are slightly larger than a pinhead and depending upon the species, may be various shapes and colors. The shell of the egg is deposited by certain glands before the egg is fertilized. Fertilization takes place through a small opening in the top of the egg. Eggs of butterflies are usually somewhat sticky when laid, thus enabling them to adhere to the plant. The

Tailed Copper

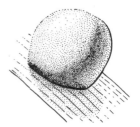

Western Tiger Swallowtail

Alfalfa Butterfly

Sonora Blue

Types of Eggs

female usually places the eggs singly or in clusters on the kind of plant that will provide suitable food for the caterpillar. This is called the *food plant.*

The larva or caterpillar that comes out of the egg looks nothing like a butterfly. It is more or less worm-like in appearance, with a very hard head, very short antennae, and eyes that are simple, not compound. Caterpillars have chewing mouthparts called mandibles. The thorax of the larva is not sharply differentiated from the rest of the body, but bears the three pairs of true legs. Five pairs of leg-like structures, called prolegs, are borne by the abdomen. They are used for locomotion and are lost when the caterpillar transforms into a pupa.

A caterpillar is born with a voracious appetite and grows very rapidly. It soon fills out its skin, or exoskeleton, to capacity. It then molts, shedding its skin and appearing in a "new suit of clothes." The new skin is formed under the old one before the old one is discarded. When the caterpillar pushes itself out of the

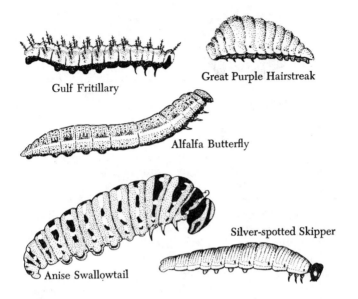

Gulf Fritillary

Great Purple Hairstreak

Alfalfa Butterfly

Silver-spotted Skipper

Anise Swallowtail

old skin, the new skin is soft and will stretch readily. The caterpillar then puffs itself up with air and grows rapidly for a few minutes. The new skin hardens and the caterpillar is now almost twice as long as it was before it molted. This process will be repeated several times before the caterpillar is full grown. When the larva reaches maximum size for the species, it will change to another very different-looking form called a pupa or chrysalid. Before transforming to the chrysalid stage, a caterpillar finds a sheltered place against a stem or branch or hanging from a leaf or fence. It then spins a small pad of silk from a spinneret on the underside of its lower lip or labium. Then it fastens the tip of its abdomen to this silken pad and proceeds to shed its skin once more. The caterpillar now becomes a compact, more-or-less cylindrical object, often protectively colored — the pupa or chrysalid. This is a

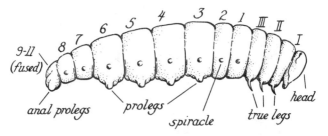

resting stage during which the insect is reorganizing physiologically to form the adult butterfly (p. 13 and p. 30).

In most cases the adult butterfly will come out in about two weeks, but pupae that form in the fall may overwinter with the butterflies emerging in the spring. When the butterfly first emerges, its wings are tiny and limp. The butterfly crawls to a convenient perch, lets its wings hang down, and slowly moves them up and down. At the same time, it pumps body juices through the wing veins. Gradually and visibly the wings get larger and larger until they reach full size. The butterfly must then wait until its wings are dry and strong before it can fly away.

Thus our butterfly has gone through its life cycle from egg to adult. This process of complete metamorphosis may be completed in a few weeks for those butterflies with several broods a year, or for the species with but one generation a year it may take most of the year.

HOW TO STUDY BUTTERFLIES

You may begin your study of butterflies with a minimum of equipment. A net of some kind is necessary. This you may purchase from a dealer (see p. 84) or make for yourself. The hoop should be of stiff wire or other metal that will not bend easily, with an opening at least twelve and preferably fifteen inches in diameter.

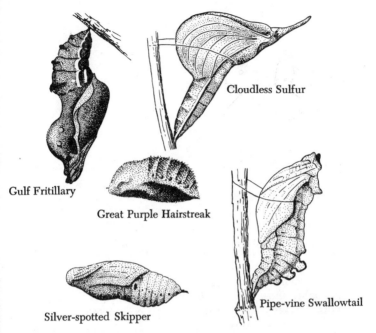

Cloudless Sulfur

Gulf Fritillary

Great Purple Hairstreak

Silver-spotted Skipper

Pipe-vine Swallowtail

The net bag should be long enough so that it will fold back over the hoop at least one and a half times when flipped and thus keep your specimens from escaping. The handle need not be more than three or four feet long. Nylon netting is generally used for insect nets today but any reasonably transparent fine-mesh netting will do.

A killing jar is essential to kill the butterflies you wish to preserve as specimens for your collection. Don't feel that the killing of insects constitutes cruelty — that is false sentimentality. Insects simply do not have the kind of nervous system that would enable them to feel pain as we know it. Also butterflies are normally short-lived and in most cases soon end up as food for other animals or are returned to the earth when they die.

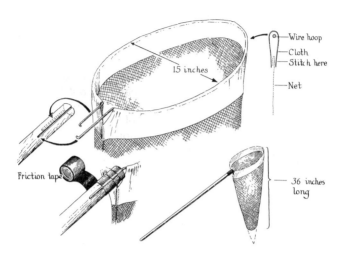

In a collector's cabinet they may bring pleasure to their owner for many years and they may also provide valuable scientific information. A cyanide killing jar is probably most satisfactory for the serious collector. It kills quickly, leaves the specimen completely relaxed, and lasts a long time. Cyanide is a deadly poison, however, and jars containing this chemical must be handled very carefully. Cyanide jars can be purchased from a dealer such as those listed on page 84.

Perhaps more satisfactory for most collectors, and recommended for use by children, is a killing jar which uses ethyl acetate or carbon tetrachloride. This jar you may make for yourself. First put about an inch of fine sawdust in the bottom of a wide-mouth pint or quart jar with a screw-top. Cover the sawdust with about a half inch of plaster of paris, made by adding water to the plaster while stirring until the mixture is about the thickness of a milkshake. Before the plaster hardens completely, push a wire through to the sawdust in several places leaving a series of small holes. When the plaster has dried thoroughly (one or two nights should be sufficient), your bottle is ready to be "charged" with a killing fluid. Ethyl acetate is preferred by most but carbon tetrachloride is more readily available and is satisfactory. Use a medicine dropper to drip the chemical down the holes in the plaster until the sawdust has absorbed as much as it can. Do not put too much or it will damage the wings of your butterflies. Tear narrow strips of paper towel or newspaper to place in the jar to absorb excess moisture and to help keep your specimens separated. Replace the lid and your bottle is ready to use. Ordinarily it will need to be "recharged" before each field trip.

Do not remove your specimens from the killing jar too soon or they will revive, but butterflies left in too long may discolor or develop stains. Five to ten minutes should be sufficient for most killing jars. Often butterflies will die with the wings turned back over the legs. To reverse them, place the butterfly on the palm of your hand and then with the forceps press the body of the butterfly gently on each side of the legs. If the insect is not too dry, the wings will usually flip back into position readily. This procedure may seem difficult at first but will become easy with practice.

A canvas bag or knapsack is useful for carrying your collecting gear — killing jar, forceps, paper envelopes, a can or box to protect the papered specimens, alcohol, vials, pill boxes, and any other items needed for your day's trip.

In using your net to catch butterflies it is often better to use a backhand stroke, since this allows you to get closer to the butterfly before swinging the net. For the most part you will have better luck catching butterflies as they light on flowers or other perches than if you chase them. Be sure to keep your eyes on the butterfly and follow its course into the net. After the butterfly is in the net, turn the net half over so that the butterfly cannot escape. Then take the lid off the killing jar, introduce the jar into the net, bring the jar under the butter-

To knock out the butterfly squeeze on the thorax

Plaster of Paris
sawdust
cyanide or
cotton with carbon-tet.

fly and cover it with the jar. Now stretch the netting tightly over the top of the jar so that the butterfly cannot get out. Then bring the lid of the killing jar into the net and slip it gently over the jar. This may sound difficult but with practice it becomes automatic.

Butterflies frequently light on the ground to sun themselves or they are attracted by moist sand, mud, or rotting fruit. In such situations the net can be dropped gently over the butterfly. Hold the tip of the net bag extended in your left hand as you drop the net. When you have trapped the butterfly in most cases it will fly upward into the net bag and you can then quickly swing your net in the air and proceed as before.

Many collectors, as soon as they catch the butterfly, trap it in a fold of the net with its wings folded over the back and then pinch the thorax lightly between thumb and forefinger. This stuns the specimen and it can then be placed easily in the killing jar without danger of damage to the specimen or it can be put directly in paper envelopes (see p. 17) which can be placed in the killing jar later. This procedure is not

generally recommended for if you are careless and squeeze too tightly or squeeze the abdomen instead of the thorax you may damage your specimen.

Specimens which cannot be mounted on the day they are collected or those collected as duplicates are ordinarily stored in paper triangles. These can be made up in various sizes as shown above. Glassine envelopes such as those used by stamp collectors can also be used. Always be sure to write the date and place of capture as well as the name of the collector on the envelope before you put the butterfly in it.

To prepare butterflies for your collection you will need special insect pins, glass-headed pins, strips of blotter or file card, and a spreading board. Insect pins are long, thin pins especially resistant to the corrosive action of insect body juices. They come in a variety of sizes but numbers 2 and 3 are best for most butterflies. Ordinary pins will corrode until they break in two within just a few years if used for insects. Pins with enlarged glass or plastic heads are preferred for securing the paper strips that hold the wings down. You may

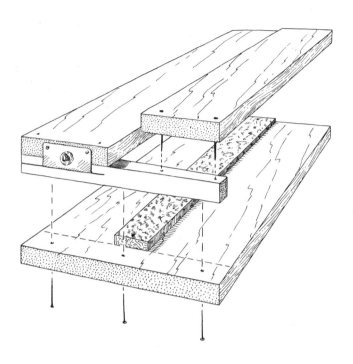

purchase a spreading board from one of the companies listed on page 84 or make your own as shown in the illustration above.

Butterflies are spread as shown on page 19. Put an insect pin through the center of the thorax between the front wings. Be sure the pin is at right angles with the body and that the specimen is about two-thirds of the way up the pin. Your specimens should stay on the board until completely dry or the wings will droop. The time necessary will vary with the temperature and humidity: a week or ten days will do in most cases. Test for dryness by touching the abdomen gently with a pin. If the abdomen is rigid the butterfly is ready to remove from the board.

The information you keep with the specimen is as important as the specimen itself. In fact, butterflies without collection data have little or no scientific value. The most important facts to record are the place and the date the specimen was collected and the name of the collector. These data are ordinarily placed on labels as shown on page 20. Labels may be hand-written or printed with a crow quill pen, printed on a small hand press (four point type recommended), or typed out, copied and reduced photographically and then printed as photographs on non-glossy but smooth photo paper. You may wish to put other information on labels also.

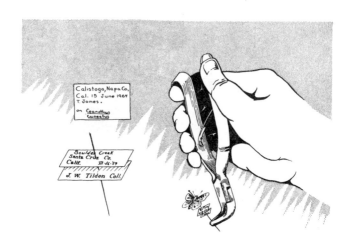

Reared specimens are always so labeled. You may add such details as the kind of flower it was visiting or other information about its habitat. If it is a specimen you have obtained by exchange from another collector you may include a label to indicate that it is now a part of your collection.

If you stockpile your duplicate specimens in paper triangles (fully labeled and identified, and stored in sealed cigar boxes containing PDB crystals or naphthalene flakes as a fumigant), sooner or later you will have enough on hand so that it will be worthwhile for you to get in touch with collectors in other areas to arrange for an exchange of duplicates. In this way you may add many new species to your collection that may not occur in your area. You will find names and addresses of collectors interested in exchanging specimens in *The Naturalists' Directory* and in the *News of the Lepidopterists' Society*. (See p. 84 for addresses of these publications.)

When you first start collecting butterflies, cigar boxes will probably be satisfactory for housing your specimens. To prepare them for use you need only glue a

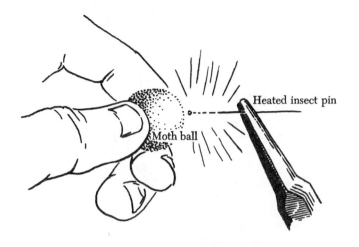

Heated insect pin

Moth ball

pinning surface to the bottom of the box. You may use cork, balsa wood, yucca pith, or Celotex. More readily available and yet satisfactory will be two sheets of a soft corrugated cardboard cut with the corrugations of one sheet running crosswise to those of the other sheet.

A cigar box collection must be inspected and fumigated frequently for the lids are obviously not pest-proof. The fumigants mentioned above for the papered specimens may be used. Also you may impale a moth ball on a heated insect pin as shown above and then place it in a corner of your insect box.

As your collection grows and becomes more valuable you may wish to purchase professional insect boxes or museum cases. These may vary in price from about three to fifteen dollars and may be obtained from one of the dealers listed on page 84.

In order to mount papered specimens you must first relax or moisten them. This is done by placing them in a relaxing or moistening chamber. A glass bell jar, set over a container of clean sand moistened with a solution made by adding a teaspoonful of carbolic acid or phenol crystals to a quart of warm water, makes an excellent relaxing chamber. If carbolic acid or phenol is not used mold will develop on your specimens and spoil them. Also quite satisfactory as a moistening chamber is a plastic refrigerator jar with sand, cotton, or clean rags moistened as above. Ordinarily it would be best to place the papered specimens on a small wooden tray or rack rather than in direct contact with the moist material. The length of time necessary for relaxing insects varies greatly for different specimens. Check by moving the wings back and forth with your forceps. When they move easily your specimen is ready for mounting.

An alternate method to drying and relaxing butterfly specimens is found in the use of chlorocresol, a crystalline chemical with the property of keeping insect specimens in a relaxed condition for indefinite periods of time. To use this method, get several plastic boxes of small size, such as 5″ x 5″ x 1½″, with tight lids. Place about a tablespoonful of chlorocresol in the bottom of a plastic box, and cover the chemical with a layer of cellucloth. Place the fresh butterfly specimens in a layer on the cellucloth, taking care they do not overlap one another. A second layer of cellucloth is then laid carefully over the specimens, and a second layer of insects may be placed on the second layer of cellucloth. This process may be continued until the box is comfortably full, so that when a final protective layer of cellucloth is placed over the specimens, they will not shift around in the box. Put the lid on tightly and the specimens will keep until you are ready to prepare them.

You may store your boxed specimens indefinitely in a refrigerator, removing specimens as needed, and returning the remainder to the refrigerator. Do not leave such boxes of specimens in exceptionally hot situations, such as open sunlight, as steaming may injure the insects. Refrigeration is not necessary if the specimens are to be prepared in a few days.

Sufficient chlorocresol for a large number of field trips may be obtained for few dollars. Some supply houses provide complete instructions with each shipment.

You may best study the life histories of butterflies and also incidentally obtain perfect specimens for your collection by rearing them in cages. You may start with the eggs, caterpillars, or chrysalids.

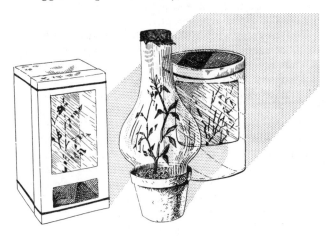

To obtain eggs you may watch the female butterfly in the field. If she proceeds from one plant to another, visiting the leaves rather than the flowers, she is probably depositing eggs on the undersides of the leaves. Follow her and collect the leaves with the eggs. Or you may place female butterflies in rearing cages containing a branch of the proper food plant set in a jar of wet sand. Suggestions for several types of rearing cages may be seen above. To keep the female alive as long as possible include fresh flowers or a bottle-cap of honey in the cage.

Caterpillars may be found on the appropriate food plants and at the right time of year for each species. See the species accounts for this information. Always keep the larvae supplied with fresh food and keep your cages clean. Some collectors use discarded nylon hose or cheesecloth to make temporary enclosures around a branch of the living food plant. With this type of rearing cage you eliminate some work but in many situations there is some risk of damage from vandals. In any case, after the larvae have pupated, remove the chrysalids to another cage to await emergence. This may vary from ten days or so to a year or more.

You may also wish to keep a collection of the different kinds of caterpillars you find. They may be preserved in vials of 70-percent alcohol. Larvae for preservation in alcohol should be killed first by dropping them in very hot water (bring water to a boil and then remove from heat). Always include in the vial a slip of paper written in soft pencil giving the locality and date collected, name of collector and the food plant, if known. Caterpillars may also be preserved for pinning by squeezing out the body contents and then inflating the skin with hot air until dry. This technique is described in detail by Harman (see p. 84).

IDENTIFYING BUTTERFLIES

You must know the name of a butterfly in order to look up information about its life history, talk intelligently about it with your friends, or arrange to exchange specimens with other collectors. You should be able to identify most butterflies collected in the San Francisco Bay region with this book. You will soon recognize all of the butterfly families on sight but at first use the key to place each specimen you collect in the correct family. If you have not previously used a key for the identification of natural history specimens consult the section on the use of keys in Arthur C. Smith's *Introduc-*

tion to the Natural History of the San Francisco Bay Region, volume 1 of the California Natural History Guides.

When you know the name of the family turn first to the color plates for that family. If there are but few species in the family and your specimen is distinctive you will have no trouble picking it out immediately. Next check the black and white plates and the illustrations found in the text along with the species accounts. Again you may be able to pick it out easily. However, if you find several species, each of which seems to resemble your specimen, turn next to the species accounts for each of these species. Read them carefully for clues as to the identity of your specimen. In most cases you will find some detail of size, color, flight habit, behavior, or geographical occurrence that will indicate which species you have. If you are still unable to determine the identity of your specimen you may then want to compare it with examples in a named collection. Such collections are maintained at the California Academy of Sciences, Golden Gate Park, San Francisco; California Insect Survey, University of California, Berkeley; San Jose State College, San Jose; and California State College at Hayward. Check with the professors or curators for assistance. Also there may be an advanced collector living in your area who would be glad to help you with difficult identifications in exchange for duplicate specimens.

Most butterflies have only minor differences in coloration between the sexes, but in the blues and coppers (family Lycaenidae) the males and females may be so unlike as to appear to be different species of insects. However in all cases the sex of a butterfly may be determined easily by an examination of its abdomen. When examined closely, preferably with a hand lens, the tip of the abdomen of the male is seen to possess a pair of "claspers." These organs are used to hold the female while mating. Also males usually have slender abdomens, ending in a tuft of hairs. Females do not have claspers, are usually larger and heavier-bodied than the males, and the abdomen usually ends in a dull point without a tuft of hairs.

Key to San Francisco Bay Region Butterfly Families

1. Antennae not forming a club . . . . Moths
— Antennae ending in a club . . . . Butterflies, 2

2. Antennal club with a terminal point or apiculus; head wide between eyes; base of antennae with a tuft of hairs or "eye-lashes" . . . . Hesperiidae, p. 58
— Antennal club simple; head narrow between eyes; no "eye-lashes" present 3

3. Front legs of both sexes reduced in size; not used for walking; carried folded close to body 4
— Front legs of females normal size, used in walking; legs of males may be reduced 6

4. Some veins of forewing swollen at base; dull-colored butterflies with eyespots . . . . Satyridae, p. 27
— No veins of forewing swollen at base 5

5. Antennae without scales above; male with a black scent pouch on hind wing; large orange-brown butterflies with black veins . . . . Danaidae, p. 29
— Antennae with scales; males without scent pouch; small to large, often brightly colored . . . . Nymphalidae, p. 30

6. Antennae curved; large butterflies, in most cases with tails on the hind wings . . . . Papilionidae, p. 53
— Antennae straight; medium to small butterflies; if tails present on hind wings they are very tiny 7

7. Base of antennae not touching eyes; moderate sized white or yellow with dark markings . . . . Pieridae, p. 44
— Base of antennae touching eyes; small butterflies; often bright blue or copper-colored 8

8. Antennae two-thirds as long as anterior margin of one front wing; single species in our area black and dull red, with many white spots . . . . Riodinidae, p. 42
— Antennae shorter, about one-half as long as anterior margin of one front wing; colors blue, gray, brown, or coppery; tiny hair-like tails on the hind wings of some species . . . . Lycaenidae, p. 43

BAY REGION BUTTERFLIES: SPECIES ACCOUNTS

Grass Nymphs, Satyrs, and Ringlets
(Family Satyridae)

Small to medium-sized dull-colored butterflies, often with eye spots (round eye-like markings) on the wings, and with some of the veins at the base of the forewings swollen. *Egg* dome shaped, flattened on top. *Caterpillar* cylindrical, smooth, with posterior end notched. *Chrysalis* smooth, suspended head down by posterior end. Flight of adults bouncing.

California Ringlet

California Ringlet *(Coenonympha california)*. This little plain-colored ringlet is one of our commonest butterflies and one of the least conspicuous. It is found almost everywhere in the Bay Region and flies from spring until fall. Later broods are a bit more yellowish than the spring brood. *Early stages: egg* dome-shaped; flattened on top and with a small button in the center; *caterpillar* pale green streaked with brown; posterior end of body notched; *chrysalis* pale green or brown. *Food plants:* grasses. Three or four broods a year.

Ox-eyed Satyr *(Cercyonis pegala boopis)*. This dark, odd-looking butterfly usually excites interest in those who see it for the first time. There are on the forewing two eye-spots that are most conspicuous from the under side. Compared to the Woodland Satyr it is larger and

[27]

darker. It flies around moist meadows and marshy lagoons in June and July, and is the western subspecies of a species found from the Atlantic to the Pacific. *Early stages:* Not well known for the West. For eastern subspecies: *egg* barrel-shaped and ribbed; *caterpillar* pale green with four light stripes; *chrysalis* pale green. *Food plants:* grasses. One brood a year.

Sthenele Satyr (*Cercyonis sthenele sthenele*). This satyr formerly lived on the San Francisco Peninsula. It is now extinct. A few specimens still exist in museums. Illustrated in Holland's Butterfly Book and in Comstock's Butterflies of California. It has an irregular dark band on the underside of the hind wing. The two following subspecies still occur in California.

Woodland Satyr (*Cercyonis sthenele silvestris*). This little satyr is found in the Oak Woodland association. It is inconspicuous and often overlooked. It takes refuge in shrubbery when disturbed. It is smaller and grayer than the Ox-eyed Satyr and is found in drier places. *Food plants:* grasses. One brood, May–June.

Paula's Satyr (*C. s. paula*). Behr's Satyr (*C. behrii*), described from Marin County, is now considered a synonym of *C. s. paula*. The type specimens of *C. behrii* were destroyed in the San Francisco earthquake and fire. No similar specimens have been taken in Marin County. The types may have been mislabelled. Paula's Satyr is found in eastern California and in the Great Basin.

Iduna Arctic (*Oeneis nevadensis iduna*). This species enters our region only in the Fort Ross area of Sonoma County, and north. It is a large clay-colored butterfly that flies in openings in coniferous forest. It is considered a collector's prize. *Early stages:* almost unknown, but arctic larvae in general are known to feed on grasses.

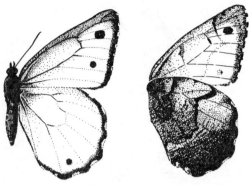

Iduna Arctic

MILKWEED BUTTERFLIES (FAMILY DANAIDAE)

The Monarch *(Danaus plexippus).* In addition to being one of the best known of our butterflies, the Monarch has the distinction of being protected by a city ordinance. In Pacific Grove, where it overwinters in great numbers, it is expressly protected. The Monarch is our only member of a family that is largely tropical. It cannot live through cold winters, and with the coming of chilly weather it migrates south. Adults pass the winter at many places along the Pacific Coast. The best known of these places is the one at Pacific Grove, where thousands may be seen on the famous Butterfly Trees. When spring returns, they move north, and eventually either they or their descendants may go as far as southern Canada. The individuals that return in the fall are probably the descendants of those that migrated north in the spring. This problem is under study and one day we will know more about the migrations of the Monarch than we now do. *Early stages: egg* pale green, higher than wide, and with vertical ribs; *caterpillar*

Prepupa

Pupa

Pupation of Monarch

dull green or whitish, with bands of yellow and black; ~~fleshy~~ horns (filaments) at each end; *chrysalis* short and stubby, pale green with golden spots and with stud-like projections; suspended by posterior end. *Food plants:* true milkweeds *(Asclepias)*. Several broods.

BRUSH-FOOTED BUTTERFLIES (FAMILY NYMPHALIDAE)

Small to large butterflies, front legs reduced, discal cell of hind wing open, antennae scaled above. *Egg* rounded or dome-shaped, with ribs. *Caterpillar* spiny, including spines on the head. *Chrysalis* suspended from the posterior end, often rough or knobby. A very large family including many of our best-known butterflies.

Gulf Fritillary *(Agraulis vanillae incarnata)*. This strikcing species is our representative of the longwings or heliconians. It was formerly not known to occur commonly north of Santa Barbara, but in recent years has become a common species of suburban areas in much of northern California. It may be recognized by the long front wings, the bright orange-brown color and the brilliant silver spots on the under side. It is a member of a tropical group and cannot endure very cold weather. A few unusually cold winters might cause it to become rare again in our region. *Early stages: egg* pale green, larger at top than bottom, like an inverted flask; *caterpillar* slender, reddish, with erect widely-spaced spines; *chrysalis* dark brown, oddly shaped with very large bulging wing covers. *Food plants:* various species of passion vine *(Passiflora).* Several broods each year.

Myrtle's Silverspot *(Speyeria zerene myrtleae).* The Zerene Silverspot has many subspecies, some of which are quite unlike each other in color. The true Zerene is found on the northern edge of our region. It may be taken near Hoberg's in Lake County. Myrtle's Silverspot is darker than other silverspots that occur in our region. It flies near the coast and is common in the Point Reyes area of Marin County in early July. It is much less common south of the Bay, along the coast. *Early stages:* almost unknown. One brood a year.

California Silverspot or **Crown Fritillary** *(Speyeria coronis).* This spangled beauty is a real native of our region. It was first discovered in the California Coast Ranges. Compared to Zerene it is larger and lighter. It is brighter colored and has the outer row of silver spots on the under side of the wings much narrower than the next species. By comparison with the Unsilvered Fritillary it is brightly silvered below. Males fly in June; females may be found as late as September. Coronis frequents canyons and woodland clearings. *Early stages:* Little is known about the early stages of any of our fritillaries. All have *caterpillars* that are brown and spiny, and that hide in nests in the ground by day. At night they come out to feed on wild violets.

Callippe Silverspot *(Speyeria callippe).* Our common-est fritillary, found even on the hills of San Francisco. It favors hilltops where wild pansy or Johnny-jump-up *(Viola pedunculata)* grows. South of the Bay it is a dull yellowish brown with sooty markings. The spots on the under surface are brightly silvered and the outer row on the hind wings is composed of large spots. A bright-colored subspecies called the Lilian Silverspot *(Speyeria callippe liliana)* is found north of the Bay in Napa County and farther north, with the ground color a bright reddish tan. *Early stages:* not well known; prob-ably similar to other silverspots.

Unsilvered Fritillary *(Speyeria adiaste).* This pretty insect is closely associated with the redwood forest south of the Bay, in San Mateo and Santa Cruz counties, and frequents clearings in the forest. It may be found near the town of La Honda. It is smaller and more delicate than our other fritillaries, bright reddish in color, and with very much reduced dark markings. Below the spots are not silvered. It flies in June and July. *Early stages:* nearly unknown, though the food plant is said to be Western Heartsease *(Viola ocellata),* a white and purple violet of the forest.

Western Meadow Fritillary *(Boloria epithore).* Looks like a small silverspot; about half as large. Bright orange-brown with reduced dark markings. There is a purplish-brown shade to the underside of the hind wings, and the spots are not silvered. This is not a com-mon species in our region. It flies in late May in the redwood districts, and may be found often on cut-over land. Cave Gulch near Santa Cruz is a good locality. *Early stages:* apparently unknown, but the larvae sup-posedly feed on violets.

Common Checkerspot *(Euphydryas chalcedona).* The black and white checkering of the upper surfaces, the red trim, and the pointed forewings of this common but elegant species are unmistakable. It is abundant almost everywhere. It is quite tame and may be picked from flowers by hand. There is a great deal of individual variation and very dark freaks occur. Some of these have received names, but they are only variants of the Common Checkerspot. *Early stages: egg* dome-shaped, narrower at the top, ribbed; yellow at first, later turning red; *caterpillar* black and spiny, living in colonies on the food plants; *chrysalis* ivory to lavender-gray, spotted with black and orange. *Food plants:* members of the Figwort family *(Scrophulariaceae);* Bee Plant *(Scrophularia californica),* monkey flowers *(Diplacus* and *Mimulus),* Indian Paint Brush *(Castilleia parviflora),* and others. One brood a year. Eggs hatch in early summer, the caterpillars feed for a short time and then overwinter. Development is completed the following spring.

Editha Checkerspots *(Euphydryas editha* subspecies). This checkerspot is much more local and colonial than the Common Checkerspot. It often occurs on serpentine soils and flies earlier in the year. We have two subspecies of the Editha Checkerspot in our region. The Bay-region Checkerspot *(E. editha bayensis)* is found on serpentine hills from Twin Peaks in San Francisco to San Jose or farther south, at low elevations. It flies in March and April, and occurs in large colonies, being abundant were found. Baron's Checkerspot *(E. editha baroni)* long considered to be a distinct species, is found mostly north of the Bay, in hilly places. It occurs in smaller colonies and is less common. It may be found on Black Mountain and along Huichica Creek not far from Sonoma. The Bay Region Checkerspot is duller and grayer, Baron's Checkerspot more brightly marked. Both differ from the Common Checkerspot in having shorter, more rounded wings, and much more red on the upper surface. *Early stages:* similar to those of the Common Checkerspot. *Food plants:* plantains *(Plantago).*

Northern Checkerspot (*Chlosyne palla*). Checkerspots of the genus *Melitaea* are smaller and have thinner wings than those of the genus *Euphydryas*. The Northern Checkerspot is bright rusty red with thin dark markings in the male. The females are darker, often nearly black with light markings. It is found in canyons and moist places and flies in May and June. *Early stages:* only partly known. *Caterpillar* black, spiny, with two dorsal rows of light spots. *Chrysalis* light brown. *Food plants:* said to be Indian Paint Brush (*Castilleia parviflora*).

Leanira Checkerspot (*Thessalia leanira*). Less common than our other checkerspots, occurring in local colonies. Compared to the Northern Checkerspot it is smaller, and colored black with white bands on the upper side. Below it is rather light colored with a black band across the hind wings, and with small white spots on this black band. *Early stages:* much like those of other checkerspots, as far as known. *Food plant:* recorded as a Bird's Beak (*Cordylanthus pilosus*), a member of the Figwort family.

Field Crescent (*Phyciodes campestris*). All of the Crescentspots, usually abbreviated to crescents, are small butterflies of the family Nymphalidae, and look like miniature checkerspots, but are more smoothly colored below and have a pale crescent-shaped marking near the outer edge of the hind wings, on the lower surface. The Field Crescent is a dark species, with rather heavy black markings on the upper side. It frequents fields and fence rows and flies low to the ground. It is on the wing from March to November and has several broods. *Early stages:* somewhat like those of checkerspots, with spiny caterpillars. *Food Plants:* various wild asters.

Mylitta Crescent (*Phyciodes mylitta*). Mylitta is a bright tawny little butterfly, in contrast to the dark coloration of the Field Crescent. Like the Field Crescent, Mylitta flies from early spring until fall, and has several broods. It is found almost everywhere in our region, and throughout the West. *Early stages:* incompletely known. *Caterpillar* spiny, black with yellow hairs on some of the abdominal segments. *Pupa* gray with a slight metallic sheen. *Food plants:* thistles *(Cirsium)* and milk thistle *(Silybum).* The caterpillars skeletonize the more tender leaves.

Orseis Crescent

Orseis Crescent *(Phyciodes orseis).* Orseis is regarded as a distinct species. It is larger than the Field Crescent, somewhat resembles the Mylitta Crescent in color, and has the outer edge of the hind wing wavy or slightly scalloped. It is quite rare, occurring in Marin, Napa, and Sonoma counties. The early stages seem not to have been studied.

Satyr Anglewing *(Polygonia satyrus).* A glance at these insects will show how well they deserve the popular name "anglewings." The outer edges of all four wings are incised with irregular indentations. Underneath, these butterflies look like dried leaves. The Satyr is our only common anglewing — our other species are relatively scarce or local. Anglewings live a long time as adults, and pass the winter in this stage, coming out to fly around on warm winter days. The Satyr is recognized by the browner underside, and by the lighter, more orange-brown tint of the upper surface. *Early stages:*

[35]

egg rounded, taller than wide, with about a dozen flange-like ribs; pale green; *caterpillar* covered with scattered spines; dark with a greenish-white stripe down the back; *chrysalis* wood-brown, rough and covered with tubercles (small bumps). *Food plants:* usually nettle *(Urtica).* Azalea has been recorded also. Two or more broods per year.

Rustic Anglewing *(Polygonia faunus rusticus).* A western subspecies of a species that is found in many parts of the United States and Canada. It is much more irregular or angled on the wing edges than the Satyr and the upper surface is a dark reddish color, while below there is a definite green tinge to the wings. In the east, the *food plants* of faunus have been recorded as willow, birch, and gooseberry. *Early stages:* hardly known. *Food plant:* may be azalea.

Oreas Anglewing *(Polygonia oreas).* This is a choice species, never really common. It is smaller than our other anglewings, with a rich reddish cast and with fewer dark markings, on the upper side, while the lower side is very dark and may have a slight purplish tinge. Silenus has a long period of flight, from early spring to late fall, and is likely to appear almost anywhere in our region where there are small streams. *Early stages:* seem not to have been recorded. *Food plants:* appear to be wild currant and gooseberry *(Ribes* Spp.).

Silvan Anglewing *(Polygonia silvius).* A single occurrence of this rare species is reported from the northern edge of the Bay region.

California Tortoiseshell *(Nymphalis californica).* This is one of our species that is subject to great fluctuations in numbers. Now and then there occur great outbreaks, which attract wide attention. At such times these butterflies swarm across mountain roads by the millions, covering the roads and plastering windshields and radi-

Silvan Anglewing

ators. These outbreaks are irregular. It is not known just why the numbers of this species fluctuate so widely. In many years, it may be a rather scarce butterfly. *Early stages:* apparently not fully described. *Caterpillar* spiny, black with a blue tubercle at the base of each spine and an indistinct pale line down the back. *Chrysalis* gray to pale brown, with darker markings; somewhat spiny. *Food plants:* various species of *Ceanothus,* such as wild lilac and buck brush. During outbreaks the caterpillars will eat almost any kind of plant. One or two broods a year, overwintering as adults.

Milbert's Tortoiseshell *(Nymphalis milberti furcillata).* Smaller than the California Tortoiseshell. Dark brown above with a wide band of orange-brown near the edge of the wings. In the western subspecies, this band is shaded near its inner edge with yellow. A striking butterfly, uncommon in our region, which is near the southern limits of this species. *Food plants:* usually nettle *(Urtica),* but gooseberry, willow, and sunflower have been recorded. Apparently one brood a year.

Mourning Cloak or **Camberwell Beauty** *(Nymphalis antiopa).* Few butterflies are better known or have a wider range than this distinctive species. It is found in Europe and Asia as well as in North America. It is rare

[37]

Mourning Cloak

in England, where it is called the Camberwell Beauty. Its dark color with the yellow edge is unique. When its wings are closed, it resembles a leaf, as do the angle-wings and tortoiseshells. It is a long-lived butterfly, as are many of the nymphalids, and the adults seek shelter and survive the winter. These are among the earliest butterflies to appear in the warm days of late winter and early spring. The Mourning Cloak is an easy species to raise and makes a fine insect for class displays. *Early stages: egg* green when first laid, fading whitish, then turning dark just before hatching; *Caterpillar* purplish-black, spiny, with a row of red spots at the bases of the spines along the back; *chrysalis* purplish-gray, the wing-pads brownish; spiny abdomen. *Food plants:* willow, cottonwood, and elm, possibly also other trees. Two or three broods a year.

Red Admiral or **Alderman Butterfly** (*Vanessa atalanta rubria*). This butterfly, with its dark ground color crossed by a bright red band, is like no other we have. Even the neighborhood boys know it. The red flashes brightly in flight, but the dark under surface, with its neat small eye spots, tends to conceal the butterfly when it is at rest. The adults overwinter and, like some other nymphalids, are sometimes active on warm winter days. The Red Admiral is found in both Europe and Asia as well as North America. It is not very common in our region and is quite a prize to junior collectors. *Early stages: egg* green, barrel-shaped with about ten vertical flanges; *caterpillar* black and spiny. It draws the edges of a leaf together with silk and lives inside. *Chrysalis* gray, the tubercles tipped with gold. *Food plants:* nettles (*Urtica*) and hops (*Humulus*). At least three broods. Adults may be found almost all year.

Painted Lady or **Thistle Butterfly** (*Cynthia cardui*). This is said to be the most widely distributed butterfly in the world, and has been called the **Cosmopolite**. It is native to the temperate parts of the Northern Hemisphere. In addition, man's activities have carried it to many places where it was not originally found. Like the Monarch, it is a migrant. In certain years, for example, 1952 and 1958, great migrations of Painted Ladies have crossed the deserts of southern California and these waves of butterflies have swept northward into central California and even farther north. Such flights may last for days. The individuals fly a few feet above the ground, but rise vertically over obstacles rather than going around them. Millions of individuals may be involved. The rest of the year, the Painted Lady may be found in any old lot or barnyard where thistles grow. Compared to the following two species, the Painted Lady is recognized by the white bar about two-thirds the distance from the base of the wing to the wing tip. In the West Coast Lady, this bar is orange in color. In the American Painted Lady, also called Virginia Lady, there are two very large eye-spots on the underside of the hind wing. There are many other minor differences between these species. *Early stages:*

egg green, barrel-shaped, with fourteen or more vertical ribs; *caterpillar* lavender to pale brown, with two yellowish lateral lines, below which are dark lines on each side; spiny; lives in a shelter formed by drawing leaves together with silk; *chrysalis* brown, with black dots and golden spots. *Food plants:* usually various thistles; also nettles, mallow *(Malva)*, yellow fiddleneck *(Amsinckia)*, and many other plants. Several broods.

American Painted Lady or **Virginia Lady** (*Cynthia virginiensis*). Confined to temperate America, but widely distributed there. (See above for differences between this and similar species.) *Food plants:* certain members of the Compositae, especially everlastings *(Antennaria, Gnaphalium,* etc.). Several broods a year.

West Coast Lady (*Cynthia annabella*). The only U.S. *Vanessa* restricted to the West. It also occurs south to Guatemala. Formerly confused with *Cynthia carye* of South America. Members of Cynthia were formerly included in Vanessa. The West Coast Lady looks like a smaller, more rusty edition of the Painted Lady, and is common everywhere in our region. Caterpillars may often be found in mid-winter, since our winters seldom are cold enough to halt their development. Adults may be found nearly all year. *Early stages:* egg quite similar to the preceding species; *caterpillar* variable in color from tan through brown to black with yellow lines; spiny; living in a shelter made from a leaf; *chrysalis* light to dark brown with gold flecks. *Food plants:* normally mallow *(Malva)* but has been reared from several other plants. Several broods a year. An easy species to raise in home or laboratory.

Buckeye or **Peacock Butterfly** (*Junonia coenia*). The light brown ground color with large multi-colored eye spots make a pattern that once seen will be remembered. The males may patrol a certain area that forms a sort of "territory," and will fly out and investigate every large insect that comes by. The Buckeye is common in most of our region and flies from spring until fall. The late fall specimens may be more reddish or purplish on the underside. Old neglected fields are good places to find Buckeyes, but it often occurs in city yards. *Early stages: egg* roundish, wider than high, ribbed; dark green; *caterpillar* black, often with two yellowish stripes; very spiny; *chrysalis* brown, more curved than that of the vanessas. *Food plants:* plantain *(Plantago)*, snapdragon, Monkey Flower *(Mimulus)*, and several other plants. May become a pest of cultivated snapdragons.

Lorquin's Admiral   California Sister

Lorquin's Admiral *(Limenitis lorquini).* The name of this butterfly honors Pierre Lorquin, the French collector of the gold rush days of California, who first collected this and many other species of California butterflies. Lorquin's Admiral is a showy insect, with velvety-black ground color, pure white band, and neat brick-red wing tips. It flies with a few quick wing beats alternated with gliding. It frequents stream courses and moist meadows in the hills and flies from May until fall. *Early stages: egg* nearly spherical, with raised network and short spines; silvery-green; *caterpillar* a remarkable little creature, brown, with bilobed head, two prominent horns just behind the head, and various

[41]

bumps along the back; *chrysalis* odd-shaped, with a big hump in the middle of the back; purplish-brown with light markings, the wing covers olive. *Food plants:* willow, poplar, cottonwood, cherry, and sometimes orchard trees such as prune, plum, and apple. Overwinters as a small larva in a case made of a leaf. Two or three broods a year.

California Sister *(Limenitis bredowii californica).* This is the most regal of our nymphalids, stately in flight and often seen high around forest trees. The Sister's color pattern is similar to that of Lorquin's Admiral, but the Sister is bigger, has the orange tips bordered by the ground color of the wings, and has broad bluish shadings on the underside. It seldom visits flowers, but is often attracted to water. This is one of our "flyway" butterflies, that patrols woodland paths. If you miss it on the first try, it is likely to return to its favorite perch. *Early stages: caterpillar* similar in shape to that of Lorquin's Admiral; dark green in color; *chrysalis* with a smaller hump than that of Lorquin's Admiral, and with two sharp lateral projections from the head; color, brown. *Food plants:* oaks, especially Canyon Oak and Coast Live Oak. Two or three broods. The caterpillar overwinters.

METALMARKS (FAMILY RIODINIDAE)

Small butterflies, with relatively long antennae and a spur vein in the hind wing. Closely related to the next family *(Lycaenidae)* in which they are included by some. Only one species is known to occur in our region. Largely a tropical group.

The Mormon Metalmark *(Apodemia mormo).* A small checkered butterfly, black and white with some rusty markings. Two subspecies occur in our region. The Mormon Metalmark *(A. mormo mormo)* is found in dry places in the foothills. Lange's Metalmark *(A. mormo langei)* occurs so far as we know only along the Carquinez Straits in the vicinity of Antioch, where its range is being destroyed by human settlement. Lange's Metalmark has much more rusty-red on the upper surface than the Mormon Metalmark has. *Early stages:* not well known. The larvae are very hairy. *Food plants:* wild buckwheat *(Eriogonum)*, especially the *E. latifolium* complex. One brood a year, the adults flying in late summer, July and August. Found in dry waste places, and often overlooked by collectors.

Blues, Coppers, and Hairstreaks
(Family Lycaenidae)

Small butterflies, the antennae arising from notches at the upper inner corner of the eyes. Radius (main stem vein) of the front wings with three or four branches; male with front legs reduced, those of female normal. *Egg* flattened, biscuit-shaped (said to be turban-shaped). *Caterpillar* with head partly concealed in thorax and with body flattened below; short and robust in form (said to be slug-shaped); usually covered with very short velvety hair. *Chrysalis* short and rounded, with a deep depression between the thorax and the abdomen; appressed closely to the surface where it is attached and with a strand of silk around the middle of the chrysalis.

The Lycaenidae divide nicely into three groups. **Hairstreaks** have the front wings pointed, the hind wings lobed at the anal angle, and may have short hairlike tails. The males often have a sex mark or brand on the front wing. Hairstreaks often are dull gray or brown on the upper side, but with bright markings on the hind wings below. The second group is the **Coppers** and these are larger than most lycaenids. Coppers are often metallic coppery color above, though a few are

[43]

Muir's Hairstreak	Green Hairstreak

Square-spotted Blue

dull grays. The under surface is usually covered with many small spots. There is great sexual dimorphism (differences), the females duller and more spotted than the males. The third group, the **Blues**, consists of mostly very small butterflies, with extreme differences between the males and females. The males are usually some shade of blue, while the females as a rule are dark. It would be very difficult to associate the two sexes except that the spotting of the under surfaces is similar in both sexes.

For separating the many species of Lycaenidae that occur in our region, see the tables on this family, pp. 60-71.

WHITES AND SULFURS (FAMILY PIERIDAE)

Moderate sized yellow or white butterflies with dark markings. All legs fully developed; radial and medial vein branches of front wing closely associated; some of wing colors formed from uric acid deposits; *egg* flask-shaped, taller than wide; *caterpillar* slender, smooth; *chrysalis* with head pointed and with large wing cases; attached head up and suspended by a silken girdle.

[44]

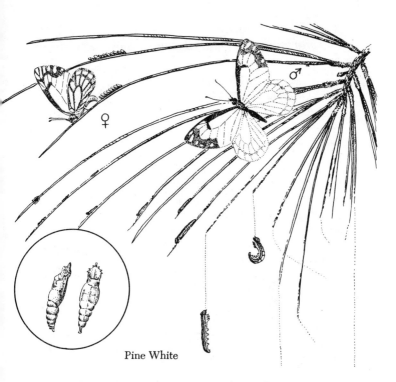

Pine White

Pine White (*Neophasia menapia*). A white butterfly about the size of the Cabbage Butterfly, with the basal two-thirds of the costal margin of the forewing black and with black markings at the tip of the forewing. It is the only member of the Pieridae in this region that is closely associated with conifers, on which the larvae feed. It is typically single-brooded, flying usually in July and August. In the Bay region it may be found in the pine and Douglas Fir forest areas of Sonoma and Napa counties. *Early stages: egg* emerald green in color, flask-shaped, fluted on sides with a circle of round beads at top; *caterpillar* dark green, with broad white band on each side and narrow white band on back; cylindrical with two short anal tails; *chrysalis* slender, dark green, with white stripes. *Food plants:*

[45]

Pinus ponderosa, Pinus contorta, and *Pseudotsuga menziesii.*

Sara Orange-tip *(Anthocaris sara).* The glimpse of an Orange-tip dashing along in the sunshine is a sure sign of spring in the Bay region. The white ground color, the reddish-orange tips of the front wings, and the mossy markings of the underside are distinctive, since this is the only Orange-tip found in our region. The spring brood has the ends of the wing veins on the hind wings black, and is more darkly marbled below. Although it is now agreed that broods do not deserve scientific names, this one was named so long ago and is so well known that the name is in general usage. This spring brood is called the Reakirt's Orange-tip. Reakirt's Orange-tip flies in March and April. The later broods are larger and lighter in color, with less marbling on the underside. These are the true Sara Orange-tip and fly in May and June. Occasionally a specimen will be quite yellowish. These are normal forms occurring now and then in the population and are not a different species. The Sara Orange-tip is distributed very widely in the Bay region. *Early stages: egg* taller than wide, with a small base; silvery green; *Caterpillar* green with a light stripe down the back; *Chrysalis* curved and pointed at the head end; either pale brown or green. *Food plants:* members of the mustard family *(Cruciferae),* especially rock cress *(Arabis)* but also ordinary mustards. At least two broods. It is believed that the chrysalis of the second brood overwinter and that the spring form emerges from these.

Boisduval's Marble *(Anthocaris lanceolata).* This species has no orange tips. The front wings are quite pointed, and the underside is very finely marbled with gray. Boisduval's Marble flies in April and May and is found in the northern part of our region. The road

Boisduval's Marble   Creusa Marble

between Mark West Springs and Calistoga is a classic collecting area for this choice insect.

Creusa Marble (*Euchloe hyantis*). This species is not common in collections. It flies in the same area with Boisduval's Marble, and at the same time of the year. Compared to the Large Marble, which is common, Creusa is smaller, more silky white, and with heavier green marbling on the underside of the hind wings.

Large Marble (*Euchloe ausonides*). White above with dark markings on the tips of the front wings. Below the hind wings are marked with a mossy patchwork of green. The Large Marble is common in our region and may be found even on the floors of the valleys, in fields where mustard grows. Often the Large Marble and the Sara Orange-tip may be found together in the same field. Both have a rapid straightaway flight. *Early stages: egg* long, flask-shaped with ridges; green when first laid, becoming orange later; *caterpillar* dark green with longitudinal stripes of lighter green; covered with short hair; *chrysalis* more slender and with smaller wing cases than that of the Sara Orange-tip; brown below, cream colored above, with dark markings. *Food plants:* native and introduced mustards. Two broods a year.

Alfalfa Butterfly or **Common Sulfur** (*Colias eurytheme*). Because it found cultivated alfalfa as suitable

Large Marble ♂   Large Marble ♀   Large Marble ♂ underside

for larval food as the native plants on which it originally fed, this Common Sulfur has come to be known as the Alfalfa Butterfly, and has developed into one of the major pests of this crop. The Alfalfa Butterfly, is a native, and was not a notable pest before alfalfa became an important crop. It is extremely variable in color. The males are yellow or orange with a solid black border to both pairs of wings. The females are yellow, orange, or white with a broken border. The summer broods are the most brilliant orange color, often with a lavender sheen. The spring forms have only a faint orange tint. Several of these forms have received names; however, they are not different species but only variants of the Alfalfa Butterfly. *Early stages: egg* fusiform (cylindric and tapering evenly to each end); red or orange, darkening before hatching; *caterpillar* variable in color, light green to dark green, with pale stripes or with interrupted red lines along the sides; *chrysalis* green with black points and short yellow lines, robust in form. *Food plants:* Many members of the pea and bean family, incuding alfalfa, vetch, clover, rattleweed *(Astragalus)*, and many others. Several broods a year.

Black and Gold Sulfur *(Colias occidentalis chrysomelas).* Larger than the Alfalfa Butterfly. Clear lemon or sulfur yellow with intense black borders in the male.

[48]

The female is lighter with very faint blackish borders. No trace of orange in either sex. This fine species is found in the mountains of our more northern counties. It may be taken near Hoberg's in Lake County but is not common. Apparently one brood. The early stages are very imperfectly known.

California Dog-face or **Flying Pansy** *(Colias eurydice)*. This is the State Butterfly of California and is considered by many to be our most beautiful native butterfly. The male is a rich yellow with violet reflections and the black borders outline a fanciful dog's head on each front wing. The Dog-face is well distributed in our region but is common in only a few localities. The Fairfax area of Marin County is a well-known spot for it. It is a strong flier and is often difficult to catch. The female is plain yellow with one dark spot in each front wing. The Dog-face flies usually in June and July, but occasional specimens may be taken in early spring and in the fall. *Early stages: egg* similar in form to that of the Alfalfa Butterfly; pale green; *caterpillar* dull green with black dots, a pale lateral line edged with orange and above this a dark mark on each segment; *chrysalis* curved in form with pointed head and large wing cases; bright green. *Food plant;* False Indigo *(Amorpha californica)*.

Cloudless Sulfur *(Phoebis sennae marcellina)*. This striking insect is more common in Arizona, but is found sparingly as far north as San Francisco, and has been observed to breed in San Jose. It is larger than other sulfurs of our region, and the males are a brilliant sulfur yellow, almost without dark markings. The females are duller yellow, with markings of dark gray and brown. This is a butterfly of the warmer parts of North America and its presence adds a tropical touch to our region. *Early stages:* much like those of other sulfurs. *Caterpillar* yellowish green with a yellow stripe on each side.

Chrysalis much curved, with long pointed head and extremely large wing cases. *Food plants:* Various species of senna *(cassia)*. These plants are not native to our region but are occasionally cultivated in gardens. Several broods a year. In our region it usually flies late in the season.

California White *(Pieris sisymbrii).* In spite of its name, this species is not common in most parts of California. It is, however, widely scattered, though scarce. Compared to other whites it may be known by its rather small size and the fact that the wing veins on both the upper and lower surfaces are darker than the ground color of the wings. The California White flies in April and May in our region, but appears later in the year in the higher mountains to the north and east. *Early stages:* not well known. *Food plants:* supposedly, members of the mustard family of plants. One brood a year.

Common White or **Southern Cabbage Worm** *(Pieris protodice).* In every backyard and farm lot, two white butterflies may be found most of the year. One is the Common White, a native species. The other is the Cabbage Butterfly, an introduced insect. The Common White is glossy white in the male, with the dark marking mostly on the front wings, which are quite pointed. The female is dull white with brown checkered markings. *Early stages: egg* spindle-shaped, with a few ridges; green; *caterpillar* slender, light green to deep bluish green, with four yellowish stripes and many small black dots; *chrysalis* yellowish to bluish gray, with points of pink or yellow and many small black dots. *Food plants:* Many species of mustards and related plants. Many broods a year. Usually not a very serious pest of cabbage.

[50]

California White   Western White

Western White *(Pieris occidentalis).* The Western White has been shown recently to be a distinct species, and has been reported from the Bay region. However, further study may make it necessary to drop this species from the list of Bay region butterflies. The Western White is a bit larger than the Common White, and the dark markings are often greenish gray. The females are never as brownish as those of the Common White. *Early stages: caterpillar* basically dull green, but banded with dark and light bands, giving the impression of a ringed insect, rather than a striped one. *Food plants:* mustards; not known to be different from those of the Common White. Two or three broods.

Veined White *(Pieris napi venosa).* Our local representative of a species that is found in the cooler parts of both the Old World and the New World. The Veined White frequents cool streamside habitats, and is one of our earliest butterflies to appear in the spring. Look for it from mid-February on into March. The dark veins of the underside are distinctive. The specimens taken in the Inner Coast Ranges have the dark borders of the veins smaller, and have been called the Small-veined White. The Veined White emerges from over-wintering chrysalids. The second brood, which appears in May, is not at all like the Veined White, but is very

[51]

Common White ♂

Veined White ♂

Cabbage White ♂

Common White ♀

Veined White ♀

Cabbage White ♀

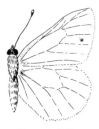

Castoria White ♂

Castoria White ♀

pale, with a few markings. This second brood is called the Castoria White, but is apparently only the second brood of the Veined White. Such brood differences are not uncommon among butterflies. *Early stages:* not very well known for our subspecies, but the life history of certain other subspecies of *Pieris napi* is well known. *Caterpillar* bright green with three yellow stripes, one on each side and one down the back. *Food plant* (of our form): milkmaids *(Dentaria)*. Two dissimilar broods a year.

Cabbage Butterfly *(Pieris rapae).* Also called the Imported Cabbage Worm, The Cabbage Butterfly is one **of the most widely known pests of cabbage and related** vegetables. It was accidentally introduced from Europe into the eastern part of North America, and has spread to all parts of the country. It is many-brooded and reproduces all year except during the very coldest weather. The Cabbage Butterfly may be separated from other white butterflies by the dull white color, the dark tips of the forewing, and the small black spot on the anterior edge of each hind wing. *Early stages: egg* pear-shaped, the small end fastened to the plant; pale green; *Caterpillar* bright green with tiny black specks; usually with a dark line down the back and yellow dots on the sides; has a velvety appearance; *chrysalis* may be either bright green or pale brown. *Food plants:* cabbage, cauliflower, and related vegetables; also many other species of native and introduced members of the mustard family.

Swallowtails and Parnassians
(Family Papilionidae)

Large butterflies; the parnassians chalky white with hind wings rounded, the swallowtails (in our region) with long tail-like projections on the hind wings. Anal margin of hind wing folded under the abdomen; antennae long and curved; *egg* nearly spherical; *cater-*

pillar with scent horns (osmateria); *chrysalis* with silken girdle (as in Pieridae) but wing cases never enlarged and with head commonly notched, not long and pointed.

Hairy Pipe-vine Swallowtail *(Battus philenor hirsuta).* No other large local butterfly is iridescent greenish-black above and has a row of red spots on the under-side of the hind wings. The Pipe-vine Swallowtail occurs over much of the central and southern United States. Its range coincides with that of its food plant, *Aristolochia.* It is found in Alameda County, Contra Costa County, and in the counties north of the Bay, but is rare or absent in most parts of Santa Clara, San Mateo, and Santa Cruz counties. This is a conspicuous, fast-flying species and one that is not easily overlooked. *Early stages: egg* spherical, rather rough; reddish brown; *caterpillar* black with bright red spots; has long fleshy filaments on the body; *Chrysalis* deep brown and somewhat S-shaped as seen from the side. *Food plant:* Dutchman's Pipe *(Aristolochia),* a vine with roundish dark green leaves and pipe-shaped brownish flowers. This Swallowtail has two or three broods a year.

Anise Swallowtail or **Western Parsley Swallowtail** *(Papilio zelicaon).* The Anise Swallowtail is the smallest of our predominantly yellow swallowtails. Its ground color is deeper yellow and the dark markings are broader. It is found in vacant lots and on roadsides as well as in the fields and hills. It may appear as early as March and in some years may be taken as late as October. It is often easier to raise caterpillars than to catch the adults. *Early stages: egg* smooth, spherical, pale green; *caterpillar* black with orange spots when young; green with black bands when mature. Will pro-trude scent horns (osmateria) from just back of the head if disturbed. *Chrysalis* either green or brown. *Food plants:* originally native parsley-like plants *(Um-*

[54]

Indra Swallowtail

belliferae); now usually found on introduced anise. Several broods a year.

Indra Swallowtail *(Papilio indra)*. A small, black swallowtail with a narrow yellow band across the wings, and tails so short as to be barely noticeable. Indra is an elegant and usually wary species, but the males often come to moist spots and are then more easily taken. Indra occurs sparingly in the northern portion of our region. *Early stages:* only partially known. *Food plant:* different members of the parsley family, which are not recorded for our region, in different parts of Indra's range.

Western Tiger Swallowtail *(Papilio rutulus)*. The bright yellow and black of the Western Tiger is a familiar sight almost anywhere in California. This is the swallowtail that most people know, flying high over streets or parks or visiting backyard flowers. It has a long flight season, from March until fall. *Early stages:* *egg* spherical, flattened at the base, deep green; *caterpillar* bright green, with big "false eyes" on the fourth segment and a black and yellow bar just back of these.

[55]

It lives in a shelter made by drawing leaves together. *Chrysalis* dark brown. Except for the Pipe-vine Swallowtail, the chrysalids of our swallowtails are quite similar. *Food plants:* several species of broad-leaved trees, such as cottonwood, elm, willow, and even certain orchard trees. Several broods a year. Adults visit water as well as flowers.

Two-tailed Swallowtail *(Papilio multicaudata).* This largest of our swallowtails is superficially similar to the Western Tiger, but has two tails on each hind wing. The black bands across the wings are relatively narrow in the Two-tailed Swallowtail, with much more yellow than black. In the Western Tiger the yellow and black bands are more nearly equal. The Two-tailed Swallowtail is more common in the Inner Coast Ranges, but is seen occasionally nearly anywhere in our region. *Early stages:* much like those of the Western Tiger Swallowtail, but the "eyes" of the caterpillar are nearly missing. *Food plants:* recorded as poplar and Wild Cherry, in our region supposedly principally Choke Cherry. At least two broods a year.

Pale Swallowtail *(Papilio eurymedon).* At first sight many take this elegant species for a washed-out version of the Western Tiger Swallowtail. Close inspection will show that the Pale Swallowtail has more pointed wings and is a more slender insect, and that the long tails have a half-twist. This is mostly a butterfly of the hills and canyons. It is attracted to water as well as to flowers, and numbers may sometimes be found on moist sandbars, their heads all facing the same way. The males, like those of certain other swallowtails, are "hill-toppers," playing around the summits of exposed hills. *Early stages: egg* spherical but flattened at base; yellow-green, often with a pink tint; *caterpillar* soft green; the "false eyes" are reduced to a few dark markings; *Chrysalis* brown, much like that of other swallowtails.

Plate 1. a, *Ox-eyed Satyr;* b, *Woodland Satyr;* c, *Monarch;* d, *Gulf Fritillary.*

Plate 2. a, *Myrtle's Silverspot;* b, *California Silverspot;* c, *Unsilvered Fritillary;* d, *Baron's Checkerspot;* e, *Bay-region Checkerspot;* f, *Mylitta Crescent;* g, *Western Meadow Fritillary;* h, *Common Checkerspot;* i, *Northern Checkerspot;* j, *Leanira Checkerspot;* k, *Field Crescent;* l, *Callipe Silverspot.*

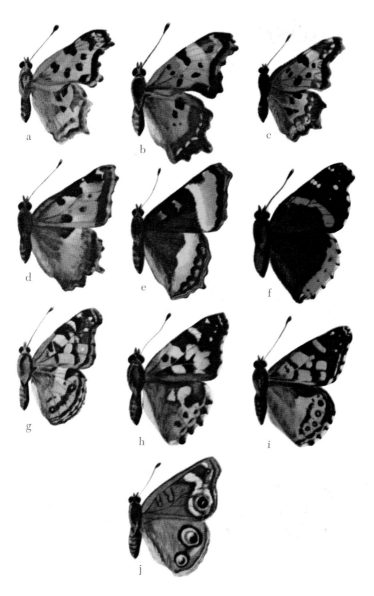

Plate 3. a, *Satyr Anglewing;* b, *Rustic Anglewing;* c, *Silenus Anglewing;* d, *California Tortoiseshell;* e, *Milbert's Tortoiseshell;* f, *Red Admiral;* g, *American Painted Lady;* h, *Painted Lady;* i, *West Coast Lady;* j, *Buckeye.*

Plate 4. a, **Mormon Metalmark**; b, **Lange's Metalmark**; c, **Great Purple Hairstreak**; d, **Thicket Hairstreak**; e, **Bramble Hairstreak**; f, **Tailed Copper**; g, **Gorgon Copper**; h, **Varied Blue**; i, **Great Copper**; j, **Purplish Copper**; k, **Marine Blue**; l, **Pygmy Blue**.

Plate 5. a, *Western Tailed Blue;* b, *Lotis Blue;* c, *Echo Blue;* d, *Melissa Blue;* e, *Greenish Blue;* f, *Mission Blue;* g, *Icarioides Blue;* h, *Pheres Blue;* i, *Acmon Blue;* j, *Arrowhead Blue;* k, *Dotted Blue;* l, *Sonoran Blue;* m, *Behr's Silver Blue;* n, *Xerces Blue;* o, *Polyphemus Blue.*

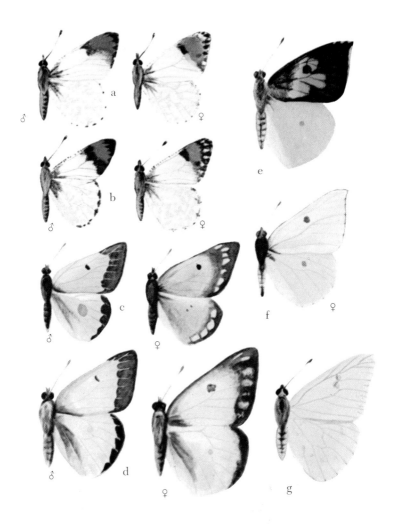

Plate 6. a, *Sara Orange-tip;* b, *Reakirt's Orange-tip;* c, *Alfalfa Butterfly;* d, *Black and Gold Sulphur;* e and f, *California Dogface;* g, *Cloudless Sulfur.*

Plate 7. a, *Western Tiger Swallowtail;* b, *Two-tailed Swallow-tail;* c, *Pale Swallowtail;* d, *Hairy Pipe-vine Swallowtail.*

Plate 8. a, *Arctic Skipper;* b, *Columbian Skipper;* c, *Lindsey's Skipper;* d, *Dodge's Skipper;* e, *Yuba Skipper;* f, *Fiery Skipper;* g, *The Sachem;* h, *Woodland Skipper;* i, *The Farmer;* j, *Yuma Skipper;* k and l *Sandhill Skipper;* m, *Siris Skipper.*

Strohbeen's Parnassian

There are at least two broods. As with our other swallowtails, the spring adults emerge from overwintering chrysalids. *Food plants:* coffee berry, also called cascara (*Rhamnus* spp.); also *Ceanothus* spp. (wild lilac, buck brush), and perhaps other plants.

Clodius Parnassian (*Parnassius clodius*). Most parnassians are found much farther north or at higher elevations than occur in our region. But Clodius flies in Marin County, Lake County, and even in Santa Cruz County, where there still exists a small colony in the Mt. Ben Lomond section. Parnassians do not look much like swallowtails, although they belong with the swallowtails structurally. Parnassians are medium-sized butterflies, chalky-white in color, without tails, and usually with a few red or orange spots on the wings. We have two subspecies of Clodius. The one north of the Bay is considered to be the true Clodius. The one in Santa Cruz County is smaller, less clearly white, and with reduced dark markings. This is Strohbeen's Parnassian (*Parnassius clodius strohbeeni*). *Early stages:* apparently never studied in our region. Most American parnassians have been found to utilize stonecrop (*Sedum*) for the larval food plants.

[57]

Roadside Skipper

Skippers (Family Hesperiidae)

Mostly small butterflies, with a very wide head and antennae far apart. Basal segment of antennae with a a tuft of hairs, forming the so-called "eye lashes." Adults with heavy bodies, short stiff wings, and rapid flight. *Egg* sea-urchin shaped to hemispherical. *Caterpillars* with prothorax small, forming a constriction or "neck" between the head and the rest of the body. *Chrysalis* usually with a slight silken cocoon. *Adults* mostly dull-colored: tan, yellowish, black, or checkered butterflies.

For separating our species of skippers, see the tables, pp. 74-83.

Tilden's Skipper

Canyon Oak Hairstreak

California Hairstreak

Common Hairstreak

Dryope Hairstreak

Woodland Hairstreak

Gray Hairstreak

Gold-hunter's Hairstreak

Hedge-row Hairstreak

Western Banded Elfin

Western Brown Elfin

NAME	ADULT BUTTERFLY
Canyon Oak Hairstreak *(Habrodais grunus lorquini)*	Brown above; yellow-brown below. Size about 1.0 in. Flight period late June–August.
Great Purple Hairstreak *(Atlides halesus corcorani)*	Iridescent blue above; red on body. Size 1.3–1.5 in. Flight period March–September.
Common Hairstreak *(Strymon melinus pudica)*	Mouse-gray above; red spots at base of tails. Size 1.0–1.2 in. Flight period March–October.
California Hairstreak *(Satyrium Californicum)*	Olive-brown above; pale marks on lower outer corner of fore wing. Dark gray below. Size 1.1–1.3 in. Flight period late May–June.
Dryope Hairstreak *(Satyrium dryope)*	Light gray-brown above; pale gray below; no tails. Size 1.1–1.3 in. Flight period June–July.
Woodland Hairstreak *(Satyrium sylvinus)*	Light olive-brown above; pale gray below; hind wing with tails. Size 1.2–1.2 in. Flight period late May–mid-July.
Gold-hunter's Hairstreak *(Satyrium auretorum)*	Deep brown above and below; small blue mark at anal angle of hind wing; fore wings pointed. Size 1.0–1.2 in. Flight period late May–June.
Gray Hairstreak *(Satyrium tetra)*	Dark gray above; below lighter gray, with light scalings. Size 1.2–1.4 in. Flight period June–July.

LYCAENIDAE
THE HAIRSTREAKS

FOOD PLANTS	HABITAT, DISTRIBUTION, AND ABUNDANCE
Oaks *(Quercus)*, esp. Canyon Live Oak.	Oak-covered ridges and canyons; distribution depends on host plant; common in favored localities.
Mistletoe *(Phoradendron)*, esp. on oak, cottonwood, and ash.	Oak woodland and stream bottoms; also in cities; never common.
Mallow, cultivated beans, lupine, hops, and many others.	Frequents flowers anywhere; distribution general; scarce early in season, later often common.
Oaks *(Quercus);* also mountain mahogany *(Cercocarpus).*	Canyons and streamsides; distribution rather general; common; visits flowers, such as those of buckeye.
Willows *(Salix).*	Streamsides mostly in the Inner Coast Ranges; distribution spotty, but species locally common.
Willows *(Salix).*	Streamsides coastwise and north of the Bay; very common where found.
Oaks *(Quercus).* Life history not well known.	Oak-covered hills of Inner Coast Ranges, both north and south of the Bay; usually quite scarce.
Hard-tack or mountain mahogany *(Cercocarpus).*	Associated with chaparral; mostly in Inner Coast Ranges both north and south of the Bay; fairly common.

NAME	ADULT BUTTERFLY
Hedge-row Hairstreak *(Satyrium saepium)*	Chestnut-brown above; wood-brown below; small blue spot at base of tail on hind wing. Size 1.0–1.1 in. Flight period June–July.
Thicket Hairstreak *(Mitoura spinetorum)*	Dull blue above; below sepia-brown with a narrow irregular white band across both pairs of wings. Size 1.0–1.2 in. Flight period irregular, May–Sept.
Muir's Hairstreak *(Mitoura nelsoni muiri)*	Dark gray with reddish-brown shades above; below dull brown with narrow light band across both pairs of wings; small spots near edge of hind wing. Size 1.0 in. Flight period late April–May.
Western Brown Elfin *(Incisalia iroides)*	Brown above and below; small projection at anal angle of each hind wing. Size 0.9–1.1 in. Flight period early spring.
Fotis Hairstreak *(Incisalia fotis)*	Male dark gray-brown, female buffy above; below with a broad very irregular dark band; hind wings scalloped. Size small, about 1.0 in. Flight period March–April.
Western Banded Elfin *(Incisalia eryphon)*	Male dark brown, female reddish-brown, above. Below light brown irregularly banded with dark brown. Outer edge of hind wing scalloped. Size 1.1–1.15 in. Flight period May–June to early July.
Bramble Hairstreak *(Callophrys dumetorum)*	Male gray, female brown, above; below yellow green; lower edge of fore wing gray. Size 1.0–1.2 in. Flight period early spring.

FOOD PLANTS	HABITAT, DISTRIBUTION, AND ABUNDANCE
Various species of *Ceanothus,* esp. Buck Brush *(C. cuneatus).*	Chaparral and forest edges; general throughout Bay region; common.
Pine Dwarfmistletoe *(Arceuthobium* spp.).	Pine and juniper forest; so far found in our region only on Mt. Diablo; rare in collections.
In nature apparently Incense Cedar *(Libocedrus decurrens)*; in laboratory has been reared on Arbor Vitae *(Thuja).*	Restricted to growths of food plant, so very local in distribution; found on Mt. St. Helena and in Mendocino Co. (near Ukiah).
Stonecrop *(Sedum)* and dodder *(Cuscuta).*	Rocky chaparral and forest edges; distribution general; locally common.
Stonecrop *(Sedum).*	Found usually near food plant; known from San Bruno hills, San Mateo Co.; scarce.
Apparently pine (*Pinus* spp.). Life history not well known.	Openings in pine forest; also in plantings of pine, as near the Presidio in San Francisco; not common.
Apparently usually Wild Buckwheat *(Eriogonum),* but *Lotis (Hosackia)* and *Syrmatium* have been recorded.	Wastelands, rocky hills, and chaparral; distribution general; common.

NAME	ADULT BUTTERFLY
Green Hairstreak (*Callophrys viridis*)	Both sexes soft gray above; blue green below; lower edge of fore wing nearly all green. Size 1.1–1.2 in. Flight period early, March–April.

THE COPPERS

NAME	ADULT BUTTERFLY
Tailed Copper (*Lycaena arota*)	Dull coppery above in male, female spotted; below brown, with many small black spots and with a light band at edge of hind wing, which is tailed. Size 1.1–1.3 in. Flight period May–June.
Gorgon Copper (*Lycaena gorgon*)	Male bright purplish copper above, female brown with yellowish dashes; below, yellowish-gray with many black spots; brick-red spots at edge of hind wing. Size 1.25–1.35 in. Flight period May–June.
Varied Blue, or Blue Copper (*Lycaena heteronea*)	Male above bright blue with narrow black rim, female duller and spotted; below, upper wings light with small black spots; lower wings silky white. Size 1.25 in. Flight period June–July.
Great Copper (*Lycaena xanthoides*)	Male coppery-gray above, female spotted; below, dull cream color with a few very small dark spots. Size 1.3–1.5 in. Flight period May–June.
Purplish Copper (*Lycaena helloides*)	Male above coppery with violet iridescence, female spotted; below orange brown, with black spots. Size 1.1–1.2 in. Flight period March–October.

FOOD PLANTS	HABITAT, DISTRIBUTION, AND ABUNDANCE
Not known for certain; probably Wild Buckwheat (*Eriogonum*).	Rocky hills near the sea; the hills of San Francisco a classic locality; limited in distribution and numbers.

THE COPPERS

Gooseberry (*Ribes*).	Restricted to vicinity of food plant; streamsides, openings in chaparral and Oak woodland; distribution general but more common in Inner Ranges.
Wild buckwheat (*Eriogonum*). In our region usually *Eriogonum latifolium nudum*.	Hillsides, cut banks and rocky outcrops where food plant grows; distribution quite general but scarce near the coast, common inland.
Several species of wild buckwheat (*Eriogonum*).	In our region restricted to certain localities north of San Francisco Bay, especially in Marin Co.; scarce in our region, common in sagebrush lands east of the Sierra Nevada.
Dock (wild rhubarb or "wild coffee") (*Rumex* spp.).	Found in fields and meadows; distribution general, often in colonies; usually common where found.
Various members of the buckwheat family-dock (*Rumex*), knotweed (*Polygonum*), etc.	Found almost everywhere, often on common knotweed in yards; very common, the most common copper in our region.

NAME	ADULT BUTTERFLY
Marine Blue *(Leptotes marina)*	Male lavender blue, two dark spots at edge of hind wing, female similar but more spotted; below gray with many small white bands. Size 1.0–1.1 in. Flight period long but irregular.
Pygmy Blue *(Brephidium exilis)*	Buffy-brown with base of wings blue; below pale brown with wavy white bands; a row of iridescent spots on outer edge of hind wing. Size tiny, 0.5–0.75 in. Flight period April–October.
Eastern Tailed Blue *(Everes comyntas)*	Male pale blue above, female usually much darker; below stone gray with small dark spots; has tails. Size small, 0.9–1.0 in. Multiple broods; flight period spring, summer, and fall.
Western Tailed Blue *(Everes amyntula)*	Male pale blue above, female duller with orange spots on hind wing; below almost white with a few small dark spots. Has tails. Size 1.0–1.2 in. or more. Flight period April–June.
Lotis Blue *(Lycaeides argyrognomon lotis)*	Deep violet blue above in male, female brown with wavy orange band across outer edge of both wings; below, this band present on both sexes, iridescent. Size 1.0–1.1 in. Flight period June.
Melissa Blue *(Lycaeides melissa)*	Much like above but lavender blue, female brown with wide orange band across both pairs of wings; below almost white, the orange band very prominent. Size 1.0 in. Flight period April and July.

FOOD PLANTS	HABITAT, DISTRIBUTION, AND ABUNDANCE
Various members of the pea family *(Leguminosae).* Life history not very well known.	Very scarce in our region; apparently most likely to occur around yards; seems to have invaded the Bay region recently.
Salt bush *(Atriplex)* lamb's quarters *(Chenopodium).*	Salt marshes, alkali flats, roadsides, and barnyards; distribution general; common, abundant in salt marshes.
Not ascertained for California. Various legumes in eastern United States.	Generally distributed but local; prefers moist swales and marshy areas; found in Inner Ranges, also in swamps in San Joaquin Valley.
Legumes, esp. vetch *(Vicia).* Prefers Giant Vetch *(Vicia gigantea).*	Canyons and woodland roadsides; found in clearings and roadsides of Redwood association.
Not known for this subspecies; thought to be *Lotis.*	Restricted to peat bogs along the immediate seacoast, known stations few; common where found; in our region reported only for Sonoma Co., possibly may occur in Marin Co.
Rattleweed *(Astragalus)* and wild licorice *(Glycyrrhiza).* Also reported on *Aster,* but this seems doubtful.	Undisturbed openings in the forest and woodland; very local but widely distributed; very rare in our region (reported only from a few localities), but common in some regions.

NAME	ADULT BUTTERFLY
Greenish Blue (*Plebejus saepiolus*)	Male cold greenish blue with wide dusky borders, female similar or else very dark brown, small spot on front wing; below, dull gray, heavily spotted with black. Size 0.9–1.1 in. Flight period May–June.
Icarioides Blue, including Mission Blue and Pheres Blue (*Plebejus icarioides* subspp.).	Male bright blue above with dark border and small black spots at edge of hind wing, female usually very dark; below stone gray with double row of black spots (East Bay) or white spots (coastal). Size 1.0–1.2 in. Flight period April–June.
Acmon Blue (*Plebejus acmon*)	Male lavender blue above with pink edge to hind wing, female very dark brown with hind wing edge orange; iridescent spots on edge of hind wing below. Size 0.8–1.0 in. Flight period February–October.
Square-spotted Blue (*Philotes battoides bernardino*)	Male cold bright violet-blue with black border, female deep brown with orange band on edge of hind wing; below, this band on both sexes, spots squarish. Size 0.75–0.9 in. Flight period June–July.
Dotted Blue (*Philotes enoptes* subspp.)	Male pale blue above with wide dusky border, female dark gray-brown with pale orange band on hind wing; spots below rounded; usually fore wing only with checkered fringes. Size 0.8–0.95 in. Flight period June, August–September.

FOOD PLANTS	HABITAT, DISTRIBUTION, AND ABUNDANCE
Certain native clovers *(Trifolium)*; also *Lotis* or *Hosackia* spp.	Cool openings and streamsides in the forest, a northern species; in our region found in cool mountain areas north of the Bay, and in cool coastal meadows (Bear Valley, Marin Co.).
Various lupines *(Lupinus)*, but apparently only the perennial species.	Four subspecies: north of the Bay *(P. i. icarioides)*; east and south of the Bay *(P. i. pardalis)*; San Francisco only *(P. i. pheres,* probably extinct); and Twin Peaks, San Francisco *(P. i. missionensis)*.
Various legumes — *Lotis, Hosackia,* etc. Also *Eriogonum* spp.	Our most common blue; found almost everywhere, from early spring until late fall.
Flat-top *(Eriogonum fasciculatum)* and several other species of *Eriogonum.*	Closely tied to food plants; found in waste lands and rocky places; rare in our region, only Marin and southern Santa Clara cos., as far as now known; more common in San Benito and Monterey cos.; an early summer species.
Late-flowering spp. of perennial *Eriogonum;* life history not well known.	Two subspecies. *P. e. bayensis:* Point Richmond, Tiburon, and other points on the Bay; June; common. *P. e. tildeni:* east of Mt. Hamilton, Santa Clara Co., and in western Stanislaus Co.; August–September; rare.

NAME	ADULT BUTTERFLY
Sonoran Blue or Red-spotted Blue (*Philotes sonorensis*)	Male silver-blue with two red spots on fore wing, female with red spots on all wings; below, dull gray with two red spots on each front wing; fringes checkered. Size 0.8–0.9 in. Flight period February–April.
Arrowhead Blue (*Glaucopsyche piasus*)	Male bright blue with dusky borders, female more dusky blue; below, stone gray with a few round black spots and white arrowhead markings on hind wing; fringes checkered. Size 1.1–1.2 in. Flight period March–early June.
Behr's Silver Blue (*Glaucopsyche lygdamus behrii*)	Male cold silver blue with narrow black borders; female brown sometimes with blue at wing base; below, both sexes, stone gray with a single line of round black spots, narrowly ringed with white, across both pairs of wings.
Xerces Blue, Polyphemus Blue (*Glaucopsyche xerces* and *G. x.* form *polyphemus*)	Male lilac blue above, female blackish; below, light gray with large round white spots (*xerces*), or black spots with white rings around them (*polyphemus*). Size 1.1–1.2 in. Flight period March–April.
Echo Blue, Spring Azure (*Celastrina argiolus echo*)	Azure blue above in male, female duller with much dusky gray on fore wing; below, whitish with tiny dark specks. Size 1.0–1.1 in. Flight period March–July (2-3 broods).

FOOD PLANTS	HABITAT, DISTRIBUTION, AND ABUNDANCE
Rock Lettuce or "Wild Hen and Chickens" *(Dudleya* or *Cotyledon).*	Found in canyons where the food plants grow (but not in all places where the plants are found); local in colonies—Alum Rock Park, Arroyo Bayo, and a few other places.
Recorded as lupine *(Lupinus).*	Cool forested areas, and along roadsides in such areas; in our region found only in the northern counties — near Hoberg's (Lake Co.) and in Sonoma and northern Napa cos.; scarce.
Leguminous plants; wild pea *(Lathyrus); Lotis scoparius;* lupine?	Borders of chaparral and woodland, and in old pastures and along roads; generally distributed; common.
Said to have been *Lotis.*	Formerly, sand dunes in San Francisco; fairly common. Now believed to be extinct.
Buds and flowers of several trees and shrubs, including dogwood *(Cornus),* buckeye *(Aesculus),* and oak *(Quercus)*	Distribution general; found almost everywhere, but commoner in wooded areas and canyons. Flies in spring and early summer; seldom seen after July 1.

[71]

underside

Northern Duskywing

Silver-spotted Skipper

♀   ♂

Common Checkered Skipper

Rural Skipper

Common Sootywing;

♂   ♀

Large Checkered Skipper

Little Checkered Skipper

[72]

Wright's Duskywing

Persius Duskywing

Funereal Duskywing

Propertius Duskywing

Grinnell's Duskywing,

Sad Duskywing

Umber Skipper

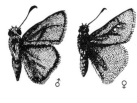

Dun Skipper

Eufala Skipper

[73]

NAME	ADULT BUTTERFLY
Silver-spotted Skipper (*Epargyreus clarus*)	Dark brown above with diagonal dull yellow row of spots on fore wing; below with large silver spot in hind wing. Size 1.75–2.25 in. Flight period May–July.
Northern Duskywing (*Thorybes pylades*)	Dark brown (not black) above, with several small light spots in outer half of fore wing; below, two faint dark bands on hind wing. Male with costal fold; fringes checkered. Size 1.2–1.4 in. May into June.
Rural Skipper or Two-banded Skipper (*Pyrgus ruralis*)	Very dark gray, checkered with white; hind wing with two complete rows of linear spots. Male with costal fold. Size 0.9–1.0 in. Flight period March, April and June.
Little Checkered Skipper (*Pyrgus scriptura*)	Similar to above but much smaller; below, hind wings much paler than fore wings. Male without costal fold. Size 0.7–0.8 in. Flight period March–April and midsummer.
Common Checkered Skipper (*Pyrgus communis*)	Male light gray, female dark gray, both with extensive checkered white markings; very similar to *scriptura* but larger. Male with costal fold. Size 0.9–1.1 in.
Large Checkered Skipper (*Heliopetes ericetorum*)	Male white with edges of wings checkered with black, female gray checkered with white; below, white with rusty markings on hind wing. Size 1.25–1.35 in., our largest checkered skipper. Flight period April–Oct.
Common Sootywing (*Pholisora catullus*)	Sooty black above and below, with tiny white dots in fore wing and in some specimens a band of white dots on hind wing. Size small, 0.8–0.9 in. Flight period March–May.

FOOD PLANTS	HABITAT, DISTRIBUTION, AND ABUNDANCE
Many kinds of leguminous plants, including locust, *Wistaria*, false indigo *(Amorpha)* and others.	Oak woodlands and openings in forest; local in our region; Mt. Cobb, Lake Co., hills back of Sonoma, Sonoma Co., and a few other places; scarce.
Leguminous plants, especially certain clovers *(Trifolium)*	Oak woodland, openings in the forest, and at edges of chaparral; widely distributed, probably in every county of the region, but not common.
Said to be members of the mallow family: recorded as Wild Hollyhock or Checker Bloom *(Sidalcea)*.	Cool fields and hilltops; scarce or lacking in the Inner Ranges, more common coastwise.
Alkali Mallow *(Sida hederacea)*.	Limited to alkali fields where the food plant grows; Contra Costa Co. has produced most of the records for our region.
Mallow *(Malva)*; perhaps other members of mallow family.	Roadsides, old fields, and waste lots; distribution general; very common, may be found almost anywhere; flies all warmer months of year.
Members of the mallow family—*Sphaeralcea*, *Malva*, etc. Also hollyhock *(Althea)*.	Widely distributed, usually in drier areas where *Sphaeralcea* grows, but may turn up almost anywhere; most common in the Inner Ranges; not abundant, but at times (April, June, September–October) fairly common. Fast flier.
Lamb's quarters *(Chenopodium)*; also reported on pigweed, tumbleweed *(Amaranthus)* and ragweed *(Ambrosia)*.	Widely distributed but uncommon in our region; mostly in drier Inner Ranges; often overlooked, very inconspicuous.

NAME	ADULT BUTTERFLY
Wright's Duskywing (*Erynnis brizo lacustra*)	Blackish-brown above and below; two obscure incomplete black bands on each fore wing. No small clear spots in fore wings. Size 1.2 in. Flight period April–May.
Persius Duskywing (*Erynnis persius*)	Dusky-black with a few clear spots in fore wing; smallest of our dark Duskywings; very difficult to recognize. Size 1.15–1.2 in. Flight period May–early July.
Grinnell's Duskywing (*Erynnis pacuvius pernigra*)	Very dark — darkest of our Duskywings; few clear spots on fore wing, which is shorter than in most similar species. Size 1.1–1.2 in. Flight period May–June.
Propertius Duskywing (*Erynnis propertius*)	Dusky blackish-brown with fore wings heavily scaled with grizzly gray; largest of our duskywings. Size 1.3–1.4 in. Flight period April–early July.
Sad Duskywing (*Erynnis tristis*)	Black above and below, with edge of hind wing white. No tibial tuft on male. Fore wing shorter than in *funeralis*. Size 1.1–1.25 in. Flight period April, June, and Sept.
Funereal Duskywing (*Erynnis zarucco funeralis*)	Quite similar to *tristis*: black with white edge to hind wing, but fore wing quite long and narrow, with brownish spot near tip. Male with tibial tuft. Size a bit larger, 1.2–1.35 in. Long flight period.
Arctic Skipper (*Carterocephalus palaemon*)	Blackish with orange spots, the only skipper that is at all like this. Flies close to ground. Size 0.8–1.0 in. Flight period May–June.

FOOD PLANTS	HABITAT, DISTRIBUTION, AND ABUNDANCE
Unknown.	Local in our region; found on mountain tops and openings in elevated chaparral; quite rare. Known localities: Mt. St. Helena, Mt. Hamilton.
Apparently unknown. Earlier reports of poplar, oak, and legumes seem to be based on misidentified butterflies.	Quite generally distributed in the more mountainous parts of our region; not usually found in warm valleys or foothills; usually rather scarce.
Unknown for our sub-species. (Reported as *Ceanothus* for *pacuvius.*)	Originally described from Marin Co. Also found in similar mountainous areas of our region, and in the Santa Lucia Mts. of Monterey Co.; usually scarce.
Various species of oaks (*Quercus*), including Coast Live Oak (*Q. agrifolia*).	Our most generally distributed duskywing; found almost everywhere in the hills and mountains; common.
Oaks (*Quercus*).	Oak woodland, forest clearings, and roadsides; distribution general; sometimes common, often scarce.
Deer Weed (*Hosackia scoparius*), alfalfa (*Medicago*), perhaps other legumes.	In our region almost restricted to the Delta and to the Inner Ranges, usually common where found; a southern species, common in the Great Valley.
Grasses.	Coldest coastal valleys and meadows; local but common where found; Marin Co. (rare); Sonoma Co. (locally common).

NAME	ADULT BUTTERFLY
Columbian Skipper (*Hesperia columbia*)	All *Hesperia* in our region are orange brown above, with long brand on fore wing of male. Best marks are on underside of hind wing: *columbia* has here a short row of white spots and one basal spot. Size 0.95–1.1 in. Flight periods May–June; September–October.
Lindsey's Skipper (*Hesperia lindseyi*)	Bright orange-brown above; underside of hind wing with irregular row of yellowish spots, and veins yellow; fringes checkered below. Size 1.05–1.15 in. Flight period late May–June.
Harpalus Skipper (*Hesperia harpalus* subspp.). Two subspecies in our area, Dodge's Skipper (*Hesperia harpalus dodgei*) and Tilden's Skipper (*H. h. tildeni*)	*H. h. dodgei:* Chocolate brown below; hind wings with large creamy spots. 1.1 in. Flight period August–October. *H. h. tildeni:* Pale above; below, dull yellow to light brown, spots small and dull. Size 0.9–1.0 in. Flight period July–October.
Yuba Skipper (*Hesperia juba*)	Dark borders of wing not blending into orange-brown ground color; stigma of male slender and curved; under surface of hind wing greenish-brown with broad irregular whitish band. Size 1.1–1.25 in. Flight period June–October.
Fiery Skipper (*Hylephila phyleus*)	Male fiery orange above with dark border, below, dull orange spotted with dusky; anal fold black; female dark above with orange-brown spots, below, dull brownish with dark markings. Size 1.1–1.2 in. Flight period from March until frost.

FOOD PLANTS	HABITAT, DISTRIBUTION, AND ABUNDANCE
Grasses.	Ridges and hilltops, local and tending to be found in colonies; found in both Inner and Outer Ranges, not found as a rule on cultivated lands.
Grasses.	Oak woodland usually, may be found in other habitats sometimes; often very abundant where found; commoner north of the Bay, but distribution quite general.
Grasses.	Local and in colonies; mostly coastwise, damp meadows and pastures; common where found but lacking from wide areas.
Unknown but almost certainly grasses.	Dry Inner Ranges; apparently all south of the Bay? Abundant in drier parts of Mt. Hamilton Range.
Apparently unknown; probably grasses.	Uncultivated grasslands and hills, in our region mostly in Inner Ranges south of the Bay, Corral Hollow, San Antonio Valley, and on into San Benito Co.; local and usually uncommon, now and then common to abundant.
Grasses, including Bermuda Grass (*Cynodon dactylon*) and lawn grass (*Poa* sp.)	Lawns, yards, fence rows, edges of swamps and marshes, old fields, etc.; general in our region wherever proper habitats exist; usually rare in undisturbed backlands, but abundant near cultivation; probably has followed Bermuda Grass wherever this weed has gone.

NAME	ADULT BUTTERFLY
The Sachem, or Field Skipper *(Atalopedes campestris)*	Male dull orange-brown with dusky borders; stigma very large, below, indistinctly marked with yellowish and dusky; female darker with two squarish small clear spots in middle of fore wing. Size 1.0–1.25 in. Flight period April–June, and in the fall.
Woodland Skipper *(Ochlodes sylvanoides)*	Male bright red-brown above, tip of stigma touching dusky wing border, below, red-brown to chocolate, with or without a pale band on hind wing; female similar but no stigma. Size 0.9–1.1 in. Flight period after mid-summer, to fall.
The Farmer *(Ochlodes agricola)*	Male above blackish with bases of wings reddish-brown, clear spots near tip of stigma; female similar but no stigma; below, both sexes, hind wing clear reddish with indistinct pale band. Size 0.8–0.9 in. Flight period May and June.
Yuma Skipper *(Ochlodes yuma)*	Bright yellowish-orange above and below, with very faint dusky borders; larger than other similar skippers; stigma of male narrow, black and prominent. Size 1.1–1.35 in. Flight periods June–July and August–September.
Sandhill Skipper *(Polites sabuleti)*	Both sexes above reddish to yellowish-brown with dusky borders; stigma of male black with a gray shade below; under side hind wing with irregular yellowish patch, veins yellowish. Size 0.8–1.0 in. Flight period late fall.

FOOD PLANTS	HABITAT, DISTRIBUTION, AND ABUNDANCE
Not well known in spite of the abundance of the species; grasses.	Old fields, roadsides, woodland meadows, and overgrown yards, sometimes lawns; may be found in undisturbed grasslands and openings in the forest; common.
Grasses, native and cultivated. Has been known to develop in golf courses.	Yards, roadsides, openings in the forest, and almost everywhere in our region; probably our most common skipper, but flies only after the middle of July and on into late fall.
Grasses; probably only native species.	Streamsides, roadsides, forest edges, and woodland meadows, seldom in yards or under cultivated conditions; common to very common; flies only in spring and early summer, not in fall.
Grasses; reported to feed on Common Reed *(Phragmites),* a very large grass of wet locations.	Moist areas and marshes, even small "oases" in arid lands; in our region restricted to the Delta region (Antioch and the Delta Islands), also in the Great Valleys; local; sometimes rare.
Grasses; has been reared from Bermuda Grass *(Cynodon dactylon),* but is also found where this grass does not grow. Reported on sedges also.	Sand dunes, roadsides, edges of marshes, old uncultivated fields, and waste lands; widely distributed; seldom abundant; may occur in March–April but the late brood (August–October) is more usually taken.

NAME	ADULT BUTTERFLY
Siris or Dog-star Skipper *(Polites sonora siris)*	Above, very dark chocolate brown with bright red-brown markings; below, almost seal-brown with prominent band of ivory spots; colors very deep and rich. Size 1.1 in. Flight period May–June.
Umber Skipper *(Paratrytone melane)*	Above, both sexes rich umber brown, bases of wings red-brown, a row of small light spots on outer third of fore wing; below, purplish-brown, with spots repeated, and pale band on hind wing. Size 1.1–1.2 in. Flight period May and September.
Dun Skipper *(Euphyes vestris)*	Both sexes very deep brown above and below; stigma of male outlined with rusty shades; female with two or three pale spots in fore wing; underside of hind wing may have indistinct pale band. Size 1.0–1.15 in. Flight period May–June.
Roadside Skipper *(Amblyscirtes vialis)*	Above, very deep brown with two or three small light spots near wing tip, below with broad purplish-gray shades; fringes checkered. Size 0.8–1.0 in. Usual flight period June.
Eufala Skipper *(Lerodea eufala)*	Gray-brown above, with several tiny white specks in fore wing; below, mouse-gray, the white specks repeated; our grayest skipper; fore wings pointed. Size 0.9–1.1 in. Long flight period, but more common in August–October.

FOOD PLANTS	HABITAT, DISTRIBUTION, AND ABUNDANCE
Not known, but must be certain grasses or possibly sedges.	Restricted to cool bleak coastal grasslands and "moorlands," Marin Co., Sonoma Co., and north; local, but common to abundant where found. Not in Inner Ranges.
Grasses; has been reared on Bermuda Grass, but occurs in many places where this grass is not found, so must also use others.	Cool streamsides, clearings in woodland, forest trails, and roadsides; less often in arid areas; rare (forested areas) to common (open woodland trails); easily overlooked.
Not well-known but apparently grasses.	Colder spots coastwise, woodland meadows, peat bogs, and "moorlands," Boulder Creek and Swanton Creek, Santa Cruz Co.; Plantation, Sonoma Co., etc.; scarce to very rare in our region.
Grasses.	Cool grassy meadows and clearings, usually in moist situations; in our region so far reported only from north of the Bay; rare and local in the Bay region.
Grasses; often associated with Bermuda Grass.	Pastures, grassy fields, fence rows, and grassier parts of the Delta Region; common in the Delta, scarce in the rest of our region; a widespread species that seems to follow Bermuda Grass.

SUGGESTED REFERENCES

Comstock, John Adams. *Butterflies of California*. Los Angeles: privately published, 1927.
Out of print but available in most libraries.

Dos Passos, Cyril F. *A Synonymic List of the Nearctic Rhopalocera*. New Haven, Conn.: The Lepidopterists' Society, 1964.

Ehrlich, Paul R. and Anne H. *How to Know the Butterflies*. Dubuque, Iowa: Wm. C. Brown Co., 1961.

Ford, E. B. *Butterflies*. New York: Macmillan, 1957.

Garth, John S., and J. W. Tilden. "Yosemite Butterflies," *Journal of Research on the Lepidoptera*, 2:1 (July, 1963), 1-96.

Harman, Ian. *Collecting Butterflies and Moths*. New York: John de Graff, 1954.

Holland, W. J. *The Butterfly Book*. New York: Doubleday, 1931.

Klots, Alexander B. *A Field Guide to the Butterflies*. Boston: Houghton Mifflin, 1951.

———. *The World of Butterflies and Moths*. New York: McGraw-Hill. [1958].

Smith, Arthur C. *Western Butterflies*. Menlo Park, Calif.: Lane Book Co., 1961.

Urquart, F. A. *The Monarch Butterfly*. Toronto: University of Toronto Press, 1960.

Journal of the Lepidopterists' Society and *News of the Lepidopterists' Society*. New Haven, Conn.
For information write Mr. George Ehle, 314 Atkins Avenue, Lancaster, Penn.

The Journal of Research on the Lepidoptera. 1140 W. Orange Grove Avenue, Arcadia, Calif.

The Naturalists' Directory, PCL Publications, Box 282, Phillipsburg, N. J.

ENTOMOLOGICAL SUPPLY HOUSES

Clair Armin, 417 Palm Avenue, Reedley, California. (Insect pins only.)

Bio-Metal Associates, P.O. Box 61, Santa Monica, California.

Ward's of California, P.O. Box 1749, Monterey, California.

Robert G. Wind, 827 Congress Avenue, Pacific Grove, California.

CHECKLIST OF BAY REGION BUTTERFLIES[*]

Family SATYRIDAE

Coenonympha california Westwood, p. 27
Cercyonis pegala ariane Boisduval, p. 27, pl. 1
Cercyonis silvestris (Edwards), p. 28, pl. 1
Cercyonis behrii (Grinnell) (believed extinct), p. 28
Cercyonis sthenele (Boisduval) (believed extinct), p. 28
Oeneis nevadensis iduna (Edwards), p. 28

Family DANAIDAE

Danaus plexippus (Linnaeus), p. 29, pl. 1

Family NYMPHALIDAE

Agraulis vanillae incarnata (Riley), p. 30, pl. 1
Speyeria zerene (Boisduval), p. 31
  a. *zerene* (Boisduval), p. 31
  b. *myrtleae* dos Passos & Grey, p. 31, pl. 2
Speyeria coronis (Behr), p. 31, pl. 2
Speyeria callippe (Boisduval), p. 32, pl. 2
  a. *callippe* (Boisduval), p. 32
  b. *liliana* (Henry Edwards), p. 32
Speyeria egleis adiaste (Edwards), p. 32, pl. 2
Boloria epithore (Edwards), p. 32, pl. 2
Euphydryas chalcedona (Doubleday), p. 32, pl. 2
Euphydryas editha (Boisduval), p. 33
  a. *bayensis* Sternitzky, p. 33, pl. 2
  b. *baroni* (Edwards), p. 33, pl. 2
Melitaea palla Boisduval, p. 34, pl. 2
Melitaea leanira Felder & Felder, p. 34, pl. 2
Phyciodes campestris (Behr), p. 34, pl. 2
Phyciodes mylitta (Edwards), p. 34, pl. 2
Phyciodes orseis (Edwards), p. 35
Polygonia satyrus (Edwards), p. 35, pl. 3
Polygonia faunus rusticus (Edwards), p. 36, pl. 3

[*] With a few exceptions, the names used in the 1964 dos Passos
checklist (see Suggested References, p. 84) have been adopted
for use in this book.

Polygonia oreas silenus (Edwards), p. 36, pl. 3
Polygonia silvius (Edwards), p. 36
Nymphalis californica (Boisduval), p. 36, pl. 3
Nymphalis milberti furcillata (Say), p. 37, pl. 3
Nymphalis antiopa (Linnaeus), p. 37
Vanessa atalanta (Linnaeus), p. 38, pl. 3
Vanessa cardui (Linnaeus), p. 39, pl. 3
Vanessa virginiensis (Drury), p. 40, pl. 3
Vanessa carye Hübner, p. 40, pl. 3
Junonia coenia Hübner, p. 40, pl. 3
Limenitis lorquini (Boisduval), p. 41
Limenitis bredowi californica (Butler), p. 42

Family RIODINIDAE

Apodemia mormo (Felder & Felder), p. 42
   a. *mormo* (Felder & Felder), p. 42, pl. 4
   b. *langei* Comstock, p. 43, pl. 4

Family LYCAENIDAE

Habrodais grunus lorquini Field, p. 60
Atlides halesus corcorani Gunder, p. 60, pl. 4
Strymon melinus pudica (Henry Edwards), p. 60
Strymon californica (Edwards), p. 60
Strymon dryope (Edwards), p. 60
Strymon sylvinus (Boisduval), p. 60
Strymon auretorum (Boisduval), p. 60
Strymon adenostomatis (Henry Edwards), p. 60
Strymon saepium Boisduval, p. 62
Mitoura spinetorum (Hewitson), p. 62, pl. 4
Mitoura nelsoni muiri (Henry Edwards), p. 62
Incisalia iroides (Boisduval), p. 62
Incisalia fotis (Strecker), p. 62
Incisalia eryphon (Boisduval), p. 62
Callophrys dumetorum (Boisduval), p. 62, pl. 4
Callophrys viridis (Edwards), p. 62
Lycaena arota (Boisduval), p. 64, pl. 4
Lycaena gorgon (Boisduval), p. 64, pl. 4
Lycaena heteronea Boisduval, p. 64, pl. 4
Lycaena xanthoides (Boisduval), p. 64, pl. 4
Lycaena helloides (Boisduval), p. 64, pl. 4
Leptotes marina (Reakirt), p. 66, pl. 4

Brephidium exilis (Boisduval), p. 66, pl. 4
Everes comyntas (Godart), p. 66
Everes amyntula (Boisduval), p. 66, pl. 5
Lycaeides argyrognomon lotis (Lintner), p. 66, pl. 5
Lycaeides melissa (Edwards), p. 66, pl. 5
Plebejus saepiolus (Boisduval), p. 68, pl. 5
Plebejus icarioides (Boisduval), p. 68
    a. *icarioides* (Boisduval), p. 68
    b. *missionensis* Hovanitz, p. 68, pl. 5
    c. *pardalis* (Behr), p. 68, pl. 5
    d. *pheres* (Boisduval), p. 68, pl. 5
Plebejus acmon (Westwood & Hewitson), p. 68, pl. 5
Philotes battoides bernardino Barnes & McDunnough, p. 68
Philotes enoptes (Boisduval), p. 68, pl. 5
    a. *bayensis* Langston, p. 68
    b. *tildeni* Langston, p. 68
Philotes sonorensis (Felder & Felder), p. 70, pl. 5
Scolitantides piasus (Boisduval), p. 70, pl. 5
Glaucopsyche lygdamus behrii (Edwards), p. 70, pl. 5
Glaucopsyche xerces Boisduval (believed to be extinct), p. 70, pl. 5
    form normal *polyphemus* (Boisduval), p. 70, pl. 5
Celastrina argiolus echo (Edwards), p. 70, pl. 5

Family PIERIDAE

Neophasia menapia tau (Scudder), p. 45
Anthocaris sara Lucas, p. 46, pl. 6
    spring brood *reakirtii* Edwards, p. 46, pl. 6
Anthocaris lanceolata Lucas, p. 46
Euchloe creusa hyantis (Edwards), p. 47
Euchloe ausonides Lucas, p. 47
Colias eurytheme Boisduval, p. 47, pl. 6
    summer brood *amphidusa* Boisduval, p. 48
Colias occidentalis chrysomelas Henry Edwards, p. 48, pl. 6
Colias eurydice Boisduval, p. 49, pl. 6
Phoebis sennae marcellina (Cramer), p. 49, pl. 6
Pieris sisymbrii Boisduval, p. 50
Pieris protodice Boisduval & Leconte, p. 50
Pieris occidentalis Reakirt, p. 51
Pieris napi venosa Scudder, p. 51
    summer brood *castoria* Reakirt, p. 53
Pieris rapae (Linnaeus), p. 53

Family PAPILIONIDAE

Battus philenor hirsuta (Skinner), p. 54, pl. 7
Papilio zelicaon Lucas, p. 54
Papilio indra Reakirt, p. 55
Papilio rutulus Lucas, p. 55, pl. 7
Papilio multicaudata Kirby, p. 56, pl. 7
Papilio eurymedon Lucas, p. 56, pl. 7
Parnassius clodius Menetries, p. 57
   a. *clodius* Menetries, p. 57
   b. *strohbeeni* Sternitzky, p. 57

Family HESPERIIDAE

Epargyreus clarus (Cramer), p. 74
Thorybes pylades (Scudder), p. 74
Pyrgus ruralis (Boisduval), p. 74
Pyrgus scriptura (Boisduval), p. 74
Pyrgus communis (Grote), p. 74
Heliopetes ericetorum (Boisduval), p. 74
Pholisora catullus (Fabricius), p. 74
Erynnis brizo lacustra (Wright), p. 76
Erynnis persius (Scudder), p. 76
Erynnis pacuvius pernigra (Grinnell), p. 76
Erynnis propertius (Scudder & Burgess), p. 76
Erynnis tristis (Boisduval), p. 76
Erynnis zarucco funeralis (Scudder & Burgess), p. 76
Carterocephalus palaemon mandan (Edwards), p. 76, pl. 8
Hesperia columbia (Scudder), p. 78, pl. 8
Hesperia lindseyi (Holland), p. 78, pl. 8
Hesperia harpalus (Edwards), p. 78
   a. *dodgei* Bell, p. 78, pl. 8
   b. *tildeni* Freeman, p. 78
Hesperia juba (Scudder), p. 78, pl. 8
Hylephila phyleus (Drury), p. 78, pl. 8
Atalopedes campestris (Boisduval), p. 80, pl. 8
Ochlodes sylvanoides (Boisduval), p. 80, pl. 8
Ochlodes agricola (Boisduval), p. 80, pl. 8
Ochlodes yuma (Edwards), p. 80, pl. 8
Polites sabuleti (Boisduval), p. 80, pl. 8
Polites sonora siris (Edwards), p. 82, pl. 8
Paratrytone melane (Edwards), p. 82
Euphyes vestris (Boisduval), p. 82
Amblyscirtes vialis (Edwards), p. 82
Lerodea eufala (Edwards), p. 82